Argue like a Lawyer

How to Inform, Influence and Persuade

Argue Like a Lawyer

How to Inform, Influence and Persuade

A Lawyer's Perspective

Simon Coath

SE

First published by Shakspeare Editorial, UK, November 2021

ISBN pbk 978-1-9196360-5-4
ISBN ebk 978-1-9196360-6-1

Cover design and typesetting www.ShakspeareEditorial.org

Printed by IngramSpark

For Moira, Harry, Florence and Hattie

Contents

Appendices

Illustrations

17 • Clarity

18 • Argument

19 • Stories

20 • Engagement

Appendix A   •   Rhetorical Notes

Appendix B   •   Presentational Tips

Preface

A Lawyer's Perspective?

A **lawyer's work requires** that preliminary fact finding and analysis is undertaken with great skill and care. This heavy responsibility calls for a forensic and measured approach. Only when the lawyer has mastered the brief is it possible to devise and advance recommendations, advice and suggested arguments.

A premise of this book is that anyone can improve their reasoning and speaking performance by focusing on the intellectual skills and advocacy strategies typically used by lawyers and other skilled speakers. These insights, including rhetoric, are seldom taught, or even included, in skills training programmes.

The reference to a lawyer's perspective gives a clear heads-up to this book's approach. It should be stressed however, that its objective is not to teach formal legal skills, nor courtroom advocacy. It is simply an opportunity to look over the shoulder of a skilled communicator, and to observe how they approach and deal with communication issues. Along the way a number of techniques, strategies and tips are considered, all of which can transform any speaker's competence and confidence.

The types of communication shortcomings addressed in this book can be evidenced in the performance of speakers at all levels of expertise. Yet such presentational evidence is only the tip of the iceberg as these problems can often impact how strategies are formulated and situations managed. The completion of this book coincided with a report from McKinsey

Management Consultants in June 2021, in which they 'Define the skills citizens will need in the future world of work' with reference to 56 DELT's (distinct elements of talent) that fall within 13 skill groups. Their reference to 'talent' goes beyond the notion of skill and includes such 'aptitudes' as 'adaptability' and 'coping with uncertainty'. A cursory glance at this book's contents and a comparison with the skill groups identified by McKinsey should enthuse the reader that its contents are relevant to the needs of this time.

Simon Coath, December 2021

Introduction

Most matters that we face in our day-to-day work are relatively trivial or straightforward and require little investigation or analysis. In most run-of-the-mill situations there is little or no factual dispute and decisions and judgements are straightforward and uncontroversial, such as which plumber to retain or what route to take to work. On other occasions it may be necessary to address more difficult and challenging scenarios, for instance, having to investigate a major catastrophe or the reasons for a business failure. These weightier investigations require careful and methodical evaluation and analysis, as any shortcomings in subsequent decisions and judgements can have serious consequences.

The first stage is to ascertain, with as much clarity as possible, precisely what has happened, or is happening. Only then can reasoned decisions be made as to what needs to be done, by whom and when. The second stage involves building a strategy or plan that addresses issues established during the first stage. The third, and crucial, stage is to decide on the best way to present the strategies or plans so that they inform, influence and persuade others. This inevitably involves the use of advocacy, that is, the ability to promote a particular cause or policy.

Argue Like a Lawyer considers the skills and strategies that lawyers use when dealing with these three stages. Each skill is relatively straightforward, easily understood and can be learnt and incorporated into a person's skill set, irrespective of their experience and seniority. The three stages are covered in three modules:

- A What Happened?
- B Building an Argument
- C Presenting an Argument and the Role of Advocacy

A good advocate is a persuasive advocate and a persuasive advocate understands the role rhetoric plays in giving an argument clout. The importance of rhetoric cannot be underestimated and reference is made to the appropriate principles and techniques within each module.

Appendix A covers a number of universal rhetorical principles that help an advocate frame, structure and deliver an argument in an engaging and persuasive way. It can be read as a stand-alone introduction to rhetoric or it can be referred to as the reader works through the three modules.

Appendices B and C cover specific advocacy situations and are referred to in the main text.

Module A
What Happened?

1 • A Lawyer's Approach to What Happened?

We all have to spend time trying to figure out what has happened or what is going on. Generally, the situation is not very important and requires little investigation. However, on occasion, the outcome can be vital and is likely to have an impact on our own or someone else's interests. In such cases the quality and reliability of our investigation is crucial. For example, police investigating a crime, teachers reviewing a student's work, or managers evaluating the success or otherwise of a project or business strategy.

Lawyers have to spend a lot of time evaluating what has happened so they can properly advise their clients. This is particularly important where they are instructed to prepare claims and reports. They understand that the value of their contribution will depend upon the quality of their understanding, and that 'rubbish in' will invariably lead to 'rubbish out'.

With their keen eye for detail and analytical skills, senior lawyers and judges are very often the first choice to chair important inquiries and investigations. The outcomes and findings of such processes are generally of real social and political importance, and it is understood that no stone should be left unturned in trying to get to the bottom of things.

Undertaking a thorough review involves fact finding, which is an active and demanding process. A passive lawyer, who relies simply on what they are told, runs the risk of not grasping the full picture nor the relevant detail. Findings and arguments built on such flimsy foundations often miss the point and fall short. A doctor will have the same concerns when conducting tests and examinations prior to a diagnosis, as will a management consultant in defining the problems they are asked to resolve.

Unlike a judge chairing an inquiry, a lawyer's approach to the fact-finding stage is influenced by their instructions and their client's interest in the process. For example, a criminal prosecutor will seek arguments that explain how the defendant committed the crime, while a defence lawyer will look for explanations that divert blame from their client. That is not to say that lawyers have closed minds to prejudicial evidence and explanations. On the contrary, they will focus carefully on conflicting evidence or events as such elements have to be explained away and not simply ignored. All evidence – good or bad – is part of the 'story' and is best incorporated into the lawyer's explanation, or case theory. It is not a persuasive strategy to simply ignore inconvenient facts and other's explanations. The topic of presenting in a way that is deemed reliable and fair is clearly important and will be returned to in some depth.

Lawyers often have to question witnesses or third parties when investigating matters, which gives them an awareness of the inherent weaknesses in people's recollections and accounts of events. They understand that each witness has a unique perspective, and thus a slightly different interpretation and recollection of what happened. These differences rarely relate to questions of integrity or a person's ability to tell the 'truth'. They reflect the simple fact that we all see things differently; sometimes slightly, sometimes at great variance, but always differently.

With this in mind, lawyers take great care when questioning potential witnesses and use high levels of listening and questioning skills. Mindful of subsequent challenges and competing recollections, they will 'bench test' people's accounts and explanations of events as they proceed. This active fact-finding process exposes weaknesses and inconsistencies at an early stage, and helps to build credibility and resilience when facing later challenges.

These matters are addressed in more detail in the chapters that follow and the skills and insights examined will assist anyone who is entrusted with trying to understand what has gone on, or is going on, so that appropriate action can be taken.

2 • Truth

'the truth, the whole truth, and nothing but the truth' part of courtroom oaths across the world

This chapter looks at what a lawyer has in mind when trying to establish what has happened, with an emphasis on the reliability of people's accounts and their recollections of events. It starts with the importance of getting a 'move on', and then tackles the thorny issue of the 'truth', and a lawyer's practical approach to the notion. It concludes with a consideration of how to assess and measure a person's credibility.

This content is relevant and important for anyone responsible for getting to the bottom of things. It is a long chapter, so it concludes with a short summary.

2.1 Fresh Evidence

Fresh evidence is 'best' evidence. A delay means losing tangible evidence, fading memories and less plausible accounts. It follows that the quicker we find out what has happened, the better. This explains why police officers investigating a serious crime and a civil aviation authority investigating an air crash, waste no time in evidence gathering. The consideration of who is responsible for a state of affairs can often be left until later.

A lawyer understands the value of getting witnesses to give statements as soon as possible. A contemporaneous account is generally given more weight than a later recollection. It is this fear of having to rely solely on old recollections that explains why lawyers, and other sensible business people, make attendance notes or timely records of their work and of any advice given as matters proceed. If such work or advice is questioned later a note written at the time has a persuasive impact. Of course, this assumes that the historic record reflects the person's recollection. There is little an advocate prefers more than cross-examining a witness on the discrepancies and inconsistencies between their present testimony and earlier notes and records.

In a similar vein, photos, plans of accident scenes and other evidence is best organised as soon as possible after the event. The desirability of video evidence helps explain the proliferation of webcams on cars and wearable bodycams on police officers to record and preserve good quality contemporaneous evidence.

In technical and more complex cases, it is often sensible to instruct an independent expert early on in the investigation to assist with preliminary enquiries. Their initial insights and findings help focus the investigation.

Finally, it is important to ensure that any physical material relevant to an investigation is preserved and not discarded or lost after the event. For example, a suit allegedly stained by a dry cleaner should be preserved as evidence, and not thrown out.

2.2 The Truth?

References to the truth often assume that everybody is clear on precisely what is meant, but the position is not always straightforward. We live in a time that has been described as a 'Post Truth Era' (Ralph Keynes 2004). As allegations and claims of *fake news*, *alternative facts*, *mis-remembering* and simple *lying*, become more prevalent, many (some of whom should know better) seem willing to lie or mislead shamelessly.

The same people often seem relaxed about passing on half-baked conspiracy theories or unfounded allegations as 'truth', without any checks. Their sole concern seems to be whether it strengthens their hand or weakens their opponent. Closely related to the phenomena of fake news is a tendency in those who wish to refute or challenge facts, to claim that they are just 'opinions' or 'fake news'. Ironically, these very same people are never slow to assert their own opinions as fact.

These depressing trends have many manifestations, not only within democracy and the role of debate, but also in the way day-to-day disputes and disagreements are addressed. The process of rational discussion and debate should always be based upon shared facts, and we all have to be vigilant to ensure that those who see no value in being honest, or are just lazy, are exposed and challenged.

In such worrying times it is some relief to see organisations and movements springing up to audit and fact check the accuracy of politicians and other public figures. It is to be hoped that calling out those who seek to mislead and lie will enable us all to enjoy a more honest form of debate and discussion. Certainly, an awareness of the tricks and techniques used by dishonest people, equips us all with the ability to check claims and assertions.

On the other side of the coin, these insights will help us frame our own claims and assertions so as not to inadvertently exaggerate or mislead others. Those who develop this skill will be perceived as reliable and honest and, as a consequence, will be persuasive. The importance of framing your argument in a neutral, honest and persuasive way is returned to in Appendices A.3 and A.6.

2.3 A Lawyer's Take On Truth

Lawyers will not spend a lot of time reflecting on the truth. After all, they are not philosophers and it is not their job to establish or prove the truth. Instead, they aim to prove their case to the level required by the court. In a civil case this means that they must show that their case is more probable than their opponent's. If they are prosecuting in a criminal case, this means that the defendant is guilty 'beyond reasonable doubt'. Therefore, lawyers have a pragmatic approach and are very mindful of the shortcomings of people's recollections. A useful metaphor that reflects these shortcomings is well illustrated by the expression 'the map is not the territory' (see Illustration 2.1).

2.4 Why Do People Have Different Recollections?

The difference in peoples' recollections rarely has anything to do with honesty and is more to do with incompetence and human frailty. People are simply not very good at accurately recalling what they have seen or experienced, as a result their accounts are often flawed. Lawyers and judges are well aware of these shortcomings and court hearings often have to focus on how reliable someone's account is. It is for this reason that a lawyer preparing a cross-examination of an opposing witness will be mindful of what factors should be taken into account in evaluating the evidence. A number of these issues are considered later, including bias, consistency, quality of perception and/or recollection, and general credibility. In the meantime, it is worth understanding the map is not the territory metaphor.

Illustration 2.1 The map is not the territory

This expression was first coined in 1931 by scientist and philosopher Alfred Korzybski. It deals with the relationship between object or subject and an individual's perception. The 'territory' is the reality (i.e. what actually happened) and the 'map' is what the witness believes and/or says happened. As a person's ability to perceive, make sense of and recall a situation is not a perfect process, lawyers understand that there are likely to be material differences between what a witness tells them about an event and what actually happened.

This map/territory phenomenon becomes very apparent when interviewing a number of different witnesses about the same event. Different witnesses are likely to have different recollections because their 'maps' vary – and there are a multitude of reasons why this is the case. Sometimes recollections are dishonest or biased, but more often they are simply affected by perception, memory and recall. A lawyer investigating a case such as an accident, who has to interview a number of witnesses, will understand, and be relatively comfortable with, small inconsistencies between individual accounts. I say relatively comfortable because the situation will not be good if there are gaping inconsistencies in different accounts on one side of the dispute. Such inconsistencies are likely to be picked up by the other side in cross-examination. However, less serious inconsistencies can be lived with and although a lawyer might ask people for clarification on such points, they will not seek to coach a witness into recalling things in a particular way. Coaching or 'grooming' often leads to embellishment or exaggeration and is almost always obvious to a third party, such as a judge. Findings that evidence has been embellished or tinkered with always weaken the credibility of the case (and the reputation of the person responsible for the embellishments).

The recognition that a third party's reconstruction of an event is invariably flawed, and cannot truly equate to the thing itself, is a useful mindset for anyone charged with getting to the bottom of things. For example, a manager conducting a review of a situation prior to reporting to the board, will generally have to evaluate competing accounts from different stakeholders, each of whom may have a different interest that shapes their individual map. Each individual map is extremely useful and, when all the maps are compared and contrasted, they provide an opportunity to synthesise and formulate a map based on the 'surveys and topography' of others.

In light of the shortcomings inherent in a single witness's recollection of contested events, lawyers recognise the importance of seeking corroboration or support for their account.

Illustration 2.2 Typical discrepancies

A lawyer knows that people seldom see things in exactly the same way; if they did there would rarely be any disputes in the first place. So, for example, it is no surprise that three witnesses who saw the same bar fight or car crash, give three separate accounts. They may agree on many elements, such as location, time or weather, but it is equally likely that they differ significantly on other matters, such as whether the man in the green hoodie was holding a knife and attacking a third party.

In contractual disputes there is often disagreement about some of the terms agreed on, such as price, delivery or quality of goods. Lawyers generally focus on these contested areas, which they call issues, knowing how important it is to identify them as soon as possible, so as to focus the lines of inquiry from the outset.

2.5 Assessing Credibility and Certitude

Lawyers look for 'certitude' (that which suggests absolute certainty or conviction) when they scrutinise and evaluate views and recollections. They need to assess both the witness's credibility and their account. It is an active process and the lawyer will not simply sit back and take everything at face value.

Typical questions include:

- How much reliance can be given to the individual's 'map'?
- Are there factors that impact upon the quality of their perception? Such as what they heard and saw.
- Is what they are saying an expression of 'opinion'? If so, is it framed as such and is it a reasonable conclusion to draw from the facts?
- Does the individual have any special expertise that makes their account more reliable?
- Are there elements that reflect on the objectivity of recollection? For instance, are they the defendant's mother?
- Is there any possibility of 'confirmation bias'? This is when an individual's recollection suggests bias from a set of prejudices, assumptions or beliefs. For example, many believe that the police are beyond reproach and incapable of any wrongdoing, while others believe they are all untrustworthy and corrupt.
- Is the individual indulging in 'wishful thinking'? That is, a desire to reach a particular conclusion that distorts the reasoning process and does not reflect the evidence.

The process of evaluation requires the use of different filters – each seeking to flesh out different strengths and weaknesses.

Some filters relate to the witness's reasoning process (see Module B). Other filters reflect on witness credibility, such as, what is there about this individual that makes them more or less reliable? Illustration 2.3 considers some preliminary issues that relate to how witnesses may frame their recollections and which hint at how reliable their recollections are likely to be.

Illustration 2.3 Credibility and Certitude

When trying to ascertain the certainty of someone's account you should listen carefully and concentrate on how they frame their understanding. For example, if someone simply asserts something to be the case by suggesting 'Fred took James's wallet', you first need to ascertain why they said it and how certain they are in their recollection.

A simple assertion that something is 'a fact' does not help you evaluate how credible the accusation is. Asking the witness why they assert this, often produces information that enables you to assess how reliable the accusation is.

So, if our witness in this case says that he is 'certain' because 'Jessie in accounts told me that Fred had taken James's wallet', it is probably the case that his contribution (alone) is of little value and that time is best spent seeing what Jessie has to say. If Jessie says, 'I saw Fred take the wallet' or 'Fred told me that he had taken it', then this direct evidence is the most compelling. However, during questioning Jessie may explain that she has no direct knowledge and that she only suspects Fred took the wallet because she knows he has a serious cash problem.

It always helps to determine how and why someone is able to offer an explanation. Does it reflect their knowledge, their belief or their opinion? How did they come to be in a position to formulate such a view? Is the view based on facts, or is it speculative? The best way to test someone's account is to question them very carefully. Chapter 4, Questioning and Active Listening, deal with some of the techniques that lawyers bring to bear on such occasions.

2.6 Full Facts

Having focused on assessing and evaluating what people tell us, we can now turn to a far easier task, related to fact finding. Facts are the building blocks of a lawyer's case or argument. We are talking here about the conventional notion of a 'fact' (i.e. that which is known to be true, or which can be proved to be true).

In light of the worrying tendency of some to invent or claim that something is a fact when it is not and cannot be a fact, it may help to focus on what is or is not factual. Illustration 2.4 may help.

Illustration 2.4 Facts?

'The USA did not put a man on the moon'

The evidence from the time (films, photographs, reports, testimony) suggests that they did, so perhaps it is safe to assume that it can be proved true.

'The Iraq War was illegal'

Many rational and sensible people claim this to be a fact. They are wrong. It is merely their opinion and/or belief. Of course it's arguable, and a debating club could find that it was illegal. But such a finding does not equate to it being a fact, any more than a jury's verdict determines whether a man is innocent or not.

'The World Bank claim that the poorest people on Earth earn only $2 a day'

I have heard this claimed but I have not checked whether the World Bank have said it. Nor have I considered other evidence that might shed light on whether it is an accurate statement. However, experience dictates that when people frame their assertions as if they were fact, the audience is more likely to believe that what they've been told is fact. Citing figures and statistics in this bold way, and claiming their authenticity by reference to a reliable and trusted organisation (such as the World Bank) is a sleight of hand often used by inscrutable advocates. Always be prepared to check out a claim before accepting its authenticity.

2.7 Agreed Facts: We Have More in Common Than That Which Divides Us

From the outset of any investigation, it is sensible to separate out and list facts from elements that are contested or disputed. Lawyers often refer to the first list as 'agreed facts' and the second list as 'disputed facts'. Generally, most of the backstory and case context will be common ground between the parties (the agreed facts). The parts that are in contention (the disputed facts) will generally form the important focus of any subsequent enquiry, negotiation or hearing. However, the agreed facts provide a foundation upon which all can agree.

2.8 Summary

This chapter looked at the difficulties inherent in trying to find out 'what happened'. A major issue relates to the fact that we all see things in a slightly different way, which makes it difficult to be absolutely certain of some things. Being mindful of this uncertainty helps us address reconstructions of events, particularly when they are contested and our investigation may become adversarial.

Much of the subject matter we investigate will be factual and therefore agreed, or capable of being agreed. To focus from the outset on building an understanding of what is agreed or not, helps to formulate a reliable and comprehensive explanation as to what happened. In reporting your findings to others it will be important to bear this is mind and chose the right 'rhetorical mode' to aid clarity (see Appendix A.6).

When reporting on a third party's views, consider whether their recollections should be described as opinion/belief or knowledge. The former suggests a subjective view while the latter suggests a more objective, fact-based view (see Appendix C.2 for top tips when interviewing or questioning a witness).

3 • Issues

'To be, or not to be: that is the question'
Hamlet, *Act 3, sc. 1, William Shakespeare*

A **first task in** any investigation or problem-solving process is to identify what issues to examine. As there may be many root causes to a problem, this is not necessarily straightforward. In addition, people often have different ideas about what needs to be looked at, when, and in what order.

Lawyers are extremely issue focused. For example, the chair of a judicial inquiry will set out an agenda of matters to be determined by the inquiry and will often seek to secure a buy-in from those with an interest in the outcome. Similarly, a trial judge will look to the advocates to agree a list of issues that require adjudication. There should be no uncertainty about what is to be investigated.

Issues require focus, clarity and resolution. To avoid matters getting out of hand (e.g. different people arguing about different things) you should try to manage the situation by setting the agenda and making it clear what needs to be resolved, when, and by whom. For example, people in control will say things such as 'where is this taking us?' or 'we can deal with that issue later' or 'we need to determine responsibility before we look at loss'.

Another problem area relates to arguments about qualitative and value-laden statements such as, 'You'll never persuade me that Bruce Springsteen is a great songwriter'. Such a position begs the question as to both Springsteen's songwriting ability and the possibility of the individual ever changing their mind. If it was decided to focus objectively on Springsteen's writing ability it would be helpful to agree first (if possible) on the characteristics of a great songwriter. In common dispute situations lawyers and the legislature have devised ways to define legal issues. For example, in sale of goods cases issues are often defined by reference to such notions as 'fit for purpose' or 'satisfactory quality'.

In contract disputes, the issues can generally be identified by thinking through the chronology and by focusing on what is and what is not agreed. Illustration 3.1 reflects a straightforward contractual problem relating to fixing a replacement engine in a car.

Illustration 3.1 A legal issue

Claimant says	Car taken to garage for new engine	Sub-sequently engine fell out	Reason engine fell out was because the engine holding nuts were inadequately tightened by garage	Cost £20,000 to repair
Defendant says	Agreed	Not disputed	Disputed. The engine fell out due an inherent weakness in mounting bracket	Not disputed
			ISSUE	

In the above case a client told his lawyer how a reconditioned engine in his vintage Bentley 'fell out' a few weeks after he had it fitted. His expert had examined the car and determined that the garage engineers had failed to properly tighten the engine holding nuts. As a consequence, the engine had vibrated and worked loose, resulting in its breaking free from its mountings. The garage challenged this explanation and claimed that the reason for the incident was an inherent weakness in the engine holding mounts. They claimed this was not apparent when they worked on the car and that, after a short time, the mounts had failed, causing the engine to come loose. From the matrix in Illustration 3.1 you can see that the only contested issue is *why* the engine came free. That is the issue both parties need to focus on as they build their cases and prepare to negotiate a settlement. If the matter goes to trial, then the judge will have to decide which party has the most convincing argument.

An ability to focus on what really matters is an important skill in whatever work we undertake. Just imagine how much easier it would be to chair a meeting if you could (with the help of a decent agenda) control the process and steer people to what needs to be discussed, when.

Illustration 3.2 is an example of someone who clearly has a well-developed intellectual skill of focusing on the issues that really matter.

Illustration 3.2 Changing the issue: tea for three

I was standing in a short queue at the National Gallery Tearooms around 3.25pm. Only about 30% of the tables were occupied. In front of me was a party of three – two elderly ladies and a teenage boy who was pushing one of them in a wheelchair. A surly-looking woman sat behind the check-in desk. The party of three approached the desk and the woman in the wheelchair announced her name and said she had made an online booking for a table for three at 3.30 pm. The surly woman looked at her computer, frowned and looked up at the elderly lady, 'Name?'

'Robinson,' replied the elderly lady. 'Mrs Agnes Robinson.'

The surly lady punched in the name and after the briefest of pauses shook her head, 'No booking here for Robinson.'

The elderly lady looked a little put out and began to root about in her handbag, 'I have a booking receipt somewhere...'

The surly lady interrupted, 'If it's not on the screen there is no booking. Simple as!'

It was the elderly lady's turn to tut as she dug deeper in her handbag for her evidence.

Recognising a standoff, the smart young man interrupted, 'Do you have a table for three available now, please?'

The surly woman looked over her shoulder at the partly occupied room and then shot a look at the young boy which suggested, 'Well it looks like it, doesn't it.'

The boy then politely asked, 'Can we have a table for three now, please?'

What a smart young man! He had clearly decided that an enquiry into whether there had been a booking was a total waste of time. If the surly receptionist would simply take them to a table, the issue of whether the Tearoom or the elderly lady had got it wrong could be consigned to the waste bin of unresolved issues, where it belonged.

We should all aspire to binning as many issues as possible, and only arguing those issues that will help to resolve things.

3.1 What Issues are Relevant?

The law often determines what the issues are in a legal case. For example, in a GBH case the prosecution must prove that the defendant *intended* to cause serious harm to the victim. If the defendant denies having been present at the attack, then of course the first issue to determine is whether the defendant was there.

In non-criminal cases the factual issues are generally determined by the way in which the parties set out their arguments. For example, in the Bentley case in Illustration 3.1 there is unlikely to be any disagreement over the contractual terms, and the dispute will boil down to whether the garage was negligent in installing the engine.

In a non-legal context what we argue about is generally up to us. However, and as management gurus say, 'He who controls the agenda controls the outcome'. Clearly it is best if we are able to determine and control what issues are addressed.

Illustration 3.3 demonstrates how picking the issues enables you to control the process and how choosing a tense can switch the focus to more favourable issues. Tense is an important rhetorical technique that is addressed in Appendix A.7.

Illustration 3.3 Handling a complaint: use of tense to switch issue

I learnt that we had failed to meet the expectations of an important client in relation to reporting procedures. The client was furious and was going to call me to complain.

Clearly, the issue uppermost in my client's mind was our failure to report matters. He did not hold back in telling me just how much our failing had annoyed him. I listened very carefully to all he had to say, and I apologised. I did not rush him and waited until I felt that he had got the complaint off his chest. At that stage, my plan was to change the issue, from the specifics of this particular case, to our past dealings. To that end I expressed the hope that we had in the past – and as a general rule – met his expectations and conducted our work in a professional manner. When the client grudgingly agreed that generally our work in the past had been excellent, I decided that another shift of issue (tense) might be appropriate and asked, 'How can we prevent this type of problem ever arising again?' We then discussed and agreed some new procedures and protocols that we could adopt to avoid future reporting problems.

My strategy in this case had been to allow the client to choose the first issue, which related to culpability and blame. Such issues invariably relate to things that have happened in the past. I then moved on to consider our reputation as a general proposition, before switching the agenda to the **future**. Future issues generally involve questions of choice (e.g. there's no point going on all day long about what happened; let's look at how we can avoid this ever happening again). I often use this tense-switching strategy when trying to mediate settlements between people who are fixated by past happenings (**blame**) and who need to be steered around to what could happen in the future (**choice**).

3.2 Issues and Evidence

A judge will demand absolute clarity as to what issues the court is being asked to decide upon. Generally, the parties will be required to produce a list of the issues before the trial starts. In their opening speech the prosecution (or claimant's lawyer in a civil case) will address the issues. For example, 'My lord, there are three issues that are to be decided in this trial. The first of the three relates to what was agreed between the parties as to the rate of commission. The claimant estate agents claim that the rate agreed on this occasion was 1.5%, reflecting additional work that was required in marketing the property. The defendants deny this claim and argue that the rate payable and agreed was 1% and that this reflects the rate that was customarily agreed between the parties in their previous course of dealings. Unless I can help you further I will now turn to the second issue...'

In this example, the issue is crystal clear; was the rate 1.5% or 1.0%? The court will then want to hear about and concentrate on the evidence that helps shed light on this issue, and will not want to be distracted by irrelevant evidence.

Illustration 3.4 Top tip: identify the correct issue

When evaluating or assessing a situation, insist that those contributing to the process, focus on issues that **need** to be investigated, and ensure that contributions are relevant to that end and help you get a sense of the situation. Common difficulties include: those wishing to attack the people rather than the problem; being stuck in the wrong tense; recounting as fact that which, in reality, is opinion.

3.2.1 Straw man arguments

These arguments are very common and you should be ready to challenge them. They are a common practice among the devious and/or the muddle-headed.

A simple example of a straw man argument is when someone claims to make progress by seeking to refute an argument that is not relevant and/or is not being made.

Illustration 3.5 A straw man argument

In an anti-immigration speech, the Speaker began by setting out his premise, 'Many say that immigration can help reduce world poverty. Is that true? Well, no it's not! And let me show you why.'

His whole subsequent argument then contrasted the level of world poverty (3 billion people a day living in poverty) with the typical immigrant numbers into the USA each year (1 million). He then suggested that, as a consequence, immigration policy was not doing anything to help the poor of the world and that it would be best if the immigrants stayed where they were. The problem with this approach was that nobody was arguing that immigration into the USA was alleviating world poverty. This flawed logic meant that

the speaker had not advanced any argument to support
his anti-immigration position but had just concentrated
on attacking an argument that had not been made (the
straw man argument) At no time did he try and refute other
arguments for immigration, such as economic benefit to
country of destination or humanitarian views.

The straw man argument is a form of red herring designed
to advance the issues chosen by the proponent and to distract
from the real issues. It creates the illusion that an argument has
been refuted or defeated by the advancement of an irrelevant
proposition (the straw man), which is then refuted.

Counter straw man arguments by focusing on the issues
that need to be addressed. For example, in the immigration
argument it would be sensible to respond by not challenging
the assertion that immigration may not help the country of
origin. Such a strategy helps steal your opponent's thunder
and leaves you the space to reframe, or reset, the argument
by choosing different issues, perhaps by looking at some of
the supportive arguments, such as the benefit to the country
receiving the immigrant.

3.3 Burden and Standard of Proof

These rules concern who has to prove *what*, and *how*. In a
courtroom context they give lawyers certainty and consistency,
but non-legal fact-finding situations can also exploit these
approaches, particularly where important issues focus upon
'who' has to prove 'what', and to 'what' extent. This is why
experienced speakers often frame things with reference to
courtroom concepts. For example, in a workplace scenario a
manager might say, 'She should be entitled to the benefit of
any doubt in this case.' Or in a contractual dispute concerning

performance, 'I think we will require a high level of proof to conclude that there was any wilful neglect in this case.'

Burden and standard of proof provide two separate but connected sets of rules that address what must be proved by whom, and what standard of proof must be established for one or other party to win.

Burden of proof can be illustrated by the obligation upon the prosecution to prove their case. There is no obligation upon the defence to disprove the case or even to give evidence – which explains why many accused opt to answer police interrogators with a simple 'no comment'.

The second proposition as to standard of proof concerns the *weight* of evidence required to satisfy the court that a case has been established. Prosecutors have to prove their case *beyond a reasonable doubt*, while claimants in civil cases have to establish their case on the lower *balance of probabilities*. It should be pointed out that there are many different legal tests that relate to specific scenarios. For example, you may hear a lawyer refer to the need to show a 'prima facie case'. This refers to the need for the party alleging something to produce an *arguable case*. If a case is without any merit or substance, you might suggest that the party making the allegations have failed to produce even a 'prima facie' or arguable case.

Illustration 3.6 Top tip: issues and burden of proof

When addressing any dispute situation, it helps to have in mind the maxim, 'he who asserts must prove'. For example, although you should generally listen to a client or customer giving vent or complaining, it should be at the forefront of your mind that simply alleging something does not, of itself, equate to proving it is the case. It follows that it is generally perfectly reasonable to ask for some evidence or other proof that supports an allegation.

When presenting your own argument, you should be ready to explain how the claim has come about in a way that supports your argument. Of course, it may serve your business objectives to be seen as very supportive of people's complaints. One example is the apparent Waitrose policy of allowing refunds on returns without the customer having to justify their decision to return the goods. Such a policy is in tune with the old adage, 'the customer is always right'.

As for standard of proof, you should make others aware of the level of evidence you require in any given situation. Most of us know that Marks and Spencer require proof of purchase before making a refund or that nightclubs require strict evidence of age prior to admission. On the other hand, it might not be considered reasonable to ask to see Granny's death certificate before allowing an employee time off to attend her funeral.

The sliding scale nature of standard of proof is something lawyers have in mind when considering their cross-examination strategy and the credibility of someone's account. For example, do they wish to establish whether the witness was lying, mistaken or had simply forgotten? The standard of proof for each is different, with a higher threshold for proving that someone is lying and/or fraudulent, with lesser standards applying for claims that the witness forgot something or is mistaken.

In any event, you should desist from making allegations unless and until you are able to put up some reasoning to support that claim (see Chapter 7 for the type of reasoning required).

In addition to dispute situations these principles can be deployed in non-adversarial circumstances where management are reflecting on policy and risk. If the risk being considered is high then from a policy viewpoint it might make sense to have a lower 'burden of proof' when considering if and how to act. For example, 'If there is any question of us not being able to ship on time we should err on the side of caution and not quote on this occasion.'

Illustration 3.7 Pascal's wager

Being mindful of who has to prove what, and to what level, has practical paybacks in all manner of debates and arguments. This illustration demonstrates how a philosopher resolved his approach to a very big issue, namely, whether there is a God!

Pascal argued that it makes sense to believe in God as if you are wrong and there is no God you have lost very little. However, if you were to believe there is no God and turn out to be wrong, then the potential losses are far greater; you might miss out on going to Heaven, and may have to languish in Hell for eternity.

Variations on this type of thinking can be brought to bear on other big questions and issues. For example, what standard of proof is required on climate change before we decide to accept that it is a fact and act accordingly? Climate change sceptics may say that the standard of proof required is high. Climate change advocates may say that the standard of proof should be lower as – using Pascal's logic – the risks of ignoring the phenomena, are far greater than the risks of acting to moderate our behaviour.

3.4 Summary

When trying to get to the bottom of things, the first task should be to focus on what the issues are, which will generally be determined by the context. For example, in a contract case the contractual terms should help shine a light on what needs to be addressed (e.g. performance questions). In non-contractual cases the law often imposes obligations upon people (e.g. not to be 'negligent' when driving; not to defame people).

In many situations those in disagreement will need to define and agree the issues. Being mindful of the importance of focusing the discussion will be to your advantage. Always think about what the important issue is and how to avoid distraction by discussing and/or arguing irrelevant and non-helpful points/issues.

Illustration 3.8 Picking the issue

Mouhssin Ismail, Head of Newham Collegiate Sixth Form, was being interviewed on the day A-Level results were announced and his students had done remarkably well. A journalist asked him whether 'grade inflation' had had a bearing upon his students' success. His response was, 'There may be a debate to be had on that topic. Today is not the day!' Simply, and assertively, he sidestepped any discussion that would distract from a well-deserved focus and celebration of his pupils' achievements on that day (see Chapter 7.2.4 on kairos).

Once the issue(s) have been identified then think about who carries the burden of proof and to what standard. In non-legal cases you could suggest a standard you think is appropriate. In a dispute you could say, 'I think he should be given the benefit of the doubt' or 'I don't think this is a question of dishonesty, I think he is simply mistaken in his recollection' or 'what may or may not have been his motive is irrelevant here. I think we are best served by looking at his actions'.

4 • Questioning and Active Listening

'When you talk, you are only repeating what you already know. But if you listen, you may learn something new' Dalai Lama

People think more quickly than they speak. This can be challenging when listening to somebody who is finding it hard to articulate or explain something. The danger is that you lose patience and jump ahead of the speaker, saying things such as, 'I'm ahead of you', or 'I know what you mean'. Take care not to do this. Although it can be hard work listening to a slow, inarticulate speaker, you should try and gauge not only *what* the person is trying to tell you but also *how* effective they are in saying it. A muddled and slow explanation may indicate a muddled recollection that will carry little credibility. On the other hand, it is equally possible that such an explanation is coming from someone who is finding it hard to articulate their feelings or who is not used to being heard. A skilled listener will recognise the need for patience and of giving their witness an opportunity to tell their story.

What you should avoid in any event is seeking to improve the account by – as lawyers say – 'coaching' the witness. As discussed in Chapter 3, you should be aware of precisely what issue the speaker is seeking to address. Very often the point they have in mind is not relevant to the enquiry and then it is sensible to point this out and refocus their attention on the crucial point. There are two-stages to a successful interview or enquiry:

1. Prepare an *agenda* to keep control of the process
2. Combine a range of questioning and listening skills to obtain all the relevant information.

4.1 Agenda

In most cases, consider what issues need to be addressed before questioning begins. It helps to prepare a list of items to be discussed and to spell out the issues to the witness at the outset of the interviewing process.

People being questioned will often have their own agenda – which may not be unreasonable – but this won't help focus the process on the matters that need to be considered. For example, they may be very upset that something is not 'fair' or perhaps they are obsessed by what happened on an earlier occasion and do not feel ready to address what should happen in the future.

Setting out objectives at the start gives you a better chance of keeping control and of obtaining a clearer understanding of the situation. Of course, one must always keep an open mind and if something crops up during the listening process that changes the agenda or raises different issues, then it can be addressed.

4.2 Questioning and Active Listening Skills

Combine these complementary skill sets in an interview situation to ensure that all relevant information is obtained.

There are four key elements: forming the question, summary, clarification and reflection.

4.2.1 Question form

People often find it hard to *begin* speaking. They may be emotional or simply not know where to start. It can help if you identify a topic to discuss but it all depends upon the context. You could ask them to focus on a particular issue (e.g. 'I would like you to tell me how you felt after you learnt that the money had gone?'), or simply try to get them to relax and open up (e.g. 'Tell me something about yourself?').

It is best to ask *open* questions that invite a discursive response, such as 'Why do you want to vote for Fred?' or 'What sorts of things do you consider make a good holiday?' Too many *closed* questions, such as 'What's your name?', 'How old are you?' or 'What political party do you support?' can seem controlling and prevent someone from opening up.

Whatever the context, always keep in mind what this book will refer to as the Kipling questions, from Rudyard Kipling's poem 'I Keep Six Honest Serving Men':

> *I keep six honest serving men*
> *(They taught me all I knew);*
> *Their names are What and Why and When*
> *And How and Where and Who.*

It is worth learning these six words by heart – what, why, when, how, where and who – so they are always in the front of your mind when you ask questions.

Kipling questions are extremely useful when our questioning prompts a judgement-laden response, such as 'it was a lovely day', or 'we had a magnificent holiday'. These answers mean very little in themselves and require probing (e.g. 'Why do you say that?' or 'What do you mean by magnificent?'). What the questioner should be trying to ascertain are the facts that led to that opinion.

No discussion on question form would be complete without reference to *leading* questions, which are a lawyer's stock-in-trade when cross-examining witnesses. Leading questions suggest the answer and are put in a way that gives the witness little wriggle room. Kipling questions rarely feature in cross-examination because they give a witness the opportunity to answer in a way that suits their own agenda. By asking short, leading questions the advocate controls the witness and gets them to answer in support of the advocate's argument. The advocate only wants some degree of affirmation from the witness to the point made in the question. For example, in a debate on corporal punishment a Kipling question might be, 'Why don't you agree that juveniles should be beaten?' but an advocate might ask leading questions in the hope that each point will be agreed to (all be it reluctantly) by the witness:

- 'People, generally avoid pain, do they not?'
- 'For example, they will not touch a hot plate.'
- 'They recognise to do so will hurt them, so they avoid touching the plate.'
- 'People avoid behaviour that they recognise may lead to them suffering pain, do they not?'
- 'Being beaten causes pain, does it not?'
- 'So, it follows that the threat of suffering pain will influence a person's behaviour?'

and so on.

Such a line of questioning will not – and is not intended to – change a person's point of view. However, by setting out your reasoning in bite-sized chunks the person being questioned will have to agree with much of your reasoning, if not the conclusion. Asking leading questions is a very controlling form of questioning, so when trying to find out what actually happened the emphasis should be on trying to get the witness to expand by asking open questions. It is seldom appropriate to ask leading questions, although they may have a place, such as to clarify a point or to control a contradictory witness.

4.2.2 Summarising

A good listener will be excellent at summarising, which demonstrates that they are following precisely what the speaker has said. For example, 'So, if I'm correct, your view is that a good holiday depends on three things: weather, food and company. Is that correct?'

Summarising in this way also means you can be corrected if you've misunderstood. People can be lazy listeners, unable to summarise accurately what others have said, which means it is fair to conclude that they have not listened properly or that they are sloppy in how they make sense of what they've been told. Being able to relay what a third party has said with complete precision is a vital skill, not only for a lawyer but for us all. The skill of summarising well is described in Illustration 4.1 through a technique I call SILIS.

Illustration 4.1 SILIS: say it like it is

When summarising a third party's account do so with great care to ensure 100% accuracy. A lawyer will have this responsibility in mind when they are called upon to explain a client's situation in court. The client will be sitting behind them and the lawyer must feel confident that there are no inaccuracies in anything they say.

A similar situation applies when someone is asked to describe a scene or photograph. For example, what appears to be a young man with a tool in his hand, opening a window during the night becomes, 'I saw the burglar force his way into the house, under cover of dark – 100%!'; or a young person lying prostrate on the street outside a pub becomes, 'Deffo. I saw her absolutely drunk as a skunk and lying in the gutter.'

This is not to say that you should not invite people to form a view as to what they concluded but first get them to say what they actually saw, from a neutral position.

4.2.3 Clarifying

Active listening is about proper understanding. There will be occasions when something is not clear and further information is required (e.g. to clarify or properly understand a point). In such cases it is appropriate to halt the speaker and ask for detail. This is where Kipling questions will help. It is useful to play back part of what you've heard before asking a clarifying question. For example, 'You say this was early on in the relationship, can you remember precisely when?' or 'How many times did he call?'

4.2.4 Reflecting

This is about empathy and making appropriate responses. For example, when being told a tragic story, an empathetic listener demonstrates attention by reflecting back certain emotions and key facts (e.g. 'You were together for 55 years' or 'That must have been very upsetting for you'). However, take care not to say 'I understand' too much, as it is very rare to completely understand the feelings of a third party and claiming to can be construed as uncaring or patronising.

5 • Concluding and Reporting

Module **A has** addressed how a lawyer evaluates and assesses what has happened or what is going on. The process described should be familiar to anyone who is responsible for similar investigations. A key element to ascertain early on is precisely *why* there is an interest in finding out what has gone on. The clarity of response to this question will determine the levels of resources and analysis that are required.

This module has also looked at the obstacles that can frustrate the process. For example, how the subjective nature of truth affects different accounts. To facilitate a reliable account and to contribute to the fact-finding exercise, lawyers will not be passive but will actively listen and question. Lawyers know the importance of identifying the facts, often referred to as *agreed* facts.

Such skills contribute to the quality of the outcome. These skills are transferable, and relevant to, any context where a strategic review is being conducted or where an assessment of what has gone wrong (or right) needs to be made. The process of looking at what has happened is an integral part of the learning experience, and one that enlightens and enables us to move forward with policies, strategies and plans, based on solid foundations (such as agreed facts).

However, such investigative work will be of little value unless and until it is acted upon, and the remainder of this book looks at ways to use the information and insights gleaned from the investigative stage. For example, a first step may be to publish a report, or findings and recommendations, to be reflected upon by others. For a lawyer, the outcome will often be formulating arguments on behalf of a client, so Module B looks at ways in which lawyers incorporate their initial findings into these arguments.

5.1 Reporting

There is little point spending valuable time finding out what has happened if there is no process to record such findings for action or review.

Two things will be paramount at the reporting stage. First, making it clear what issues have been investigated, and second, what the outcomes are. One example of a typical outcome is a recommendation to make a claim for compensation against a third party. There are many examples and each requires a slightly different approach to setting out the findings, which is addressed in Modules B and C. At this point it suffices to say that you need to have in mind precisely what the planned outcomes are before 'putting pen to paper'. A very important consideration is whether the primary reporting objectives are to inform or to persuade? Strategies for addressing each objective and advice on how to structure an argument are in Module C (also see Appendix A.6 Rhetorical Modes).

Whatever the proposed objective, it is important to bear in mind that written records relating to findings can be disclosable to opponents if litigation ensues. This can raise legal issues best addressed by legal advisers at the investigation stage to ensure that such records will not create prejudice later. It follows that if reports are likely to be written and will include

references to prejudicial findings it is best to seek legal advice
prior to their publication.

Module B
Building an Argument

6 • What Is an Argument?

This chapter considers important elements in planning an argument. Its objective is to simplify the subject and to look how to identify opportunities for practice. Larger sections conclude with a brief summary.

6.1 What Is Arguing?

Part of the planning process involves taking into account other's arguments and, where appropriate, seeking to refute them. Knowing when to argue and when not to argue requires a clear appreciation of the distinctions between the processes in italics in Illustration 6.1.

Illustration 6.1 Arguing

Before a referee brandishes a red card, they must first **reason** why that action is appropriate, which can involve **value judgements** or **opinions** (e.g. the player cheated and dived). The referee must then **inform** the player why they are being sent off. There is no requirement for the referee to **argue** with or to try and **persuade** the player that the decision is correct. Of course, this will not necessarily stop the player from trying to **argue** with the referee, but any such **pleas** or **claims** are fruitless as there is no obligation upon the referee to **refute** the player's **argument**.

This book defines arguing as what we do when we seek to *influence and/or persuade someone toward our point of view.*

This might be a friend in a pub, voters in an election, a party to a negotiation or, for lawyers, a judge or jury in court.

Before we begin to argue we must be clear who our audience is, and how best we can engage and persuade them to our point of view, which is further discussed in Module C, Chapter 20 Engagement.

A proper argument articulates a set of *reasons and/or evidence* in support of a point of view. Arguing in this formal sense is very different from simply quarrelling or squabbling. What may have started as a proper argument can easily descend into name-calling, insults and/or abuse. Lawyers recognise that resorting to such tactics is both unprofessional and non-productive.

Verbal abuse, although it can be entertaining, rarely does much to advance an argument and is seldom experienced in court. That is not to say that abuse does not have its place elsewhere. Consider the cutting tongue of the late Christopher Hitchens as he attempted to ridicule, insult and offend Governor George Bush.

> *George W. Bush is lucky to be governor of Texas. He is unusually incurious, abnormally unintelligent, amazingly inarticulate, fantastically uncultured, extraordinarily uneducated, and apparently quite proud of all these things.*
> *(Hardball with Chris Matthews, NBC 2000)*

Hitchens supports his 'argument' (George Bush's good fortune in being governor of Texas) with premises and reasons that are both exaggerated and offensive. This type of argument is not likely to cut any ice with a neutral audience, by which I mean an audience that has an open mind. However, the argument and the way it is expressed is likely to be 'enjoyed' by a partisan audience who already hold Bush in low regard. In such a case there is little need or intent to *persuade* and the argument threshold is low, while the entertainment threshold is high. This book concentrates on the function of argument to persuade and/or influence – not to gratuitously offend nor to entertain.

6.1.1 Summary

Arguing in this book refers to the process that is directed at trying to *persuade* or *influence* others to a point of view. It is different from the meaning ascribed to an exchange in which people are insulting or abusing each other, often with no particular objective.

6.2 Do We Need to Argue?

Parents, teachers and authority figures must relish the power of being able to say, 'I am not going to argue with you!' This does not mean that they never need to argue, just that they have an option. The referee in Illustration 6.1 shows this by ordering the player to leave the pitch without engaging or arguing with the player any further.

What we need or want to say can often be conveyed as information, advice or guidance. For example, we do not need to be persuasive or argue when telling someone the time, what we'd like for supper or what is on TV. Relaying a third party's argument (as a 'messenger') does not mean that we necessarily ascribe to or support that view. Lawyers recognise the importance of appreciating when we seek simply to inform as compared to persuade. It avoids being dragged into an argument – unless that suits your purpose. Only when we are seeking an outcome in relation to a contested point do we need to argue. The very important distinction between arguing and explaining is returned to in Appendix A.6.

6.3 The Limits of Argument

In court, lawyers practice a form of *positional* argument, where they strive to be on the winning side by persuading the judge or jury that they have satisfied the appropriate burden of proof. One side wins, the other loses. It is high stakes but it is not the only outcome of an argument. Alternatives to adversarial argument may need to be considered.

For Archbishop Justin Welby 'the most bitter arguments are to be reconciled, not won' (*Financial Times*, 8 April 2021). This is worth bearing in mind, even if the argument can be 'won'. Using power over others to ensure capitulation or compliance is not winning an argument because, although the 'battle' may be won, the 'war' can continue. That is why using a collaborative approach to dispute resolution is often more constructive and allows relationships to survive. Reasoning is still required, but objectives and interests may need to be reframed with an emphasis upon conciliation, empathy and listening, and with a focus on needs as opposed to wants.

6.3.1 Summary

This book defines arguing as a process that is directed at *persuading* others to a point of view. People in a position of power do not always need to be persuasive as they can often direct or order. When called upon to speak it is essential to be mindful of your objective – whether it is to inform, advise or persuade – and to choose the appropriate rhetorical mode to achieve that objective.

6.4 Reasoned Argument

Some arguments relate to big issues, such as whether there is a God, others cover less weighty questions, such as what we should have for supper or watch on television. Whatever the argument, the prospects of success are increased by an understanding of rhetoric, in particular the *three pillars of persuasion: ethos, pathos, and logos*. These important rhetorical principles, often referred to as critical reasoning skills, are covered in Module C and detailed in Appendix A. Each element has some bearing upon the effectiveness of an argument and offers insights and techniques that enable us to *reason* our argument and attack the *reasoning* of our opponents. This section touches on *logos* and its appeal to *reason*.

There are two types of reasoned arguments: deductive and inductive.

6.4.1. Deductive argument: logical

In their quest for truth and enlightenment, philosophers rely on logical argument that applies *deductive reasoning* to arrive at a conclusion. For example:

- Reason 1 – all men are mortal
- Reason 2 – Socrates is a man
- Conclusion – *therefore* Socrates is mortal.

This form of argument, known as syllogism, is based on a supporting premise and/or reason that is either asserted or assumed to be true. If the premise or reason is *true* then it follows that the conclusion must also be true. People often aspire to argue in this way, yet their chain of reasoning or the conclusion they draw is flawed and its shortcomings make it easy for the opponent to pick apart the reasoning.

6.4.2 Inductive argument: rational

This is lawyers' territory and, as in commercial and social argument, it is seldom necessary to establish that the conclusion represents the *truth*. Instead, we should attempt to demonstrate that our argument is more compelling or persuasive than our opponent's, and that our conclusion is *more or less probable*. Whether or not we succeed generally depends upon the strength of our reasoning, that is, the reasons or premises that support our argument. It also depends upon our audience's willingness to accept our position. It should always be borne in mind that, however persuasive our argument, our opponent has the right to reject it. If we are debating before a tribunal, who should be relatively open to being persuaded, then we hope our line of reasoning will appear more appealing than our opponent's.

It is important to understand that inductive argument shares the same *shape* as deductive argument. It helps to picture the anatomy of an argument, as in the example of a couple arguing over what to watch on television – note the emotional (pathos) element:

- Reason 1 – We watched Strictly last week
- Reason 2 – You know I hate it
- Reason 3 – It's my birthday today
- Conclusion – Therefore we should watch X Factor tonight!

It helps to think of reasoning as the *explanation* for your *conclusion*. Good quality reasoning demonstrates that you have thought through the process and arrived at a conclusion that is probable/persuasive.

6.4.3 Summary

Argument deploys a structure in which an advocate puts forward reasons in support of their argument and invites an audience (or opponent) to reach a particular conclusion on that basis.

6.5 The Language of Argument

We have seen that an argument is an attempt to persuade someone to our point of view or conclusion. Its structure typically comprises a number of reasons or premises, followed by such words as *therefore*, *because*, *it follows*, or *so*, and then a statement of the conclusion.

Reasons can be expressed in the form of *generalisations*, *assumptions*, *inferences*, *claims*, *evidence* and *judgements*. Each of these is considered in more detail in the following chapters but it may help at this stage to illustrate the different types of reason in support of an argument that proposes flogging juvenile delinquents.

A flogging argument based on deterrent:

3. People generally avoid behaviour that causes them pain (*generalisation*)
4. Flogging will cause pain (*assumption*)
5. Most people will avoid behaviour that they know may result in them suffering pain (*generalisation/inference*).

Therefore, juveniles should be punished by flogging and this will act as a deterrent to them and to others (Chapter 4 illustrates how such an argument can be advanced in cross-examination).

A flogging argument based on economics:

1. It is expensive to incarcerate juveniles (*claim/ assumption*)
2. In 2015 the Government spent £600 million on juvenile imprisonment (*evidence*)
3. Flogging young offenders will be quick and cheap (*value judgement*)
4. Money will be saved if we flog as opposed to imprison (*assumption*).

Therefore, juveniles should be flogged, as this will be cheaper than other solutions.

An argument is only as strong as its weakest reason, like a link in a chain. The reasons chosen and the way they are described often determine whether an argument will succeed.

The purpose of this section is to demonstrate the shape and anatomy of a basic argument and to identify some important terms and concepts that relate to 'reasons' and that need to be fully understood. A glossary will suffice as a summary by helping you to understand these terms. The best way of internalising them is to use them in your day-to-day speech and to identify when others are using them. One statement can be an example of several terms, so don't get hung up on trying to fit everything into a category. For example, if I say, 'Arsenal are the greatest football team of all time' I'm making a claim, opinion and value judgement all at the same time. If someone suggests that it is a fact, they are wrong. They might then say, 'Let me tell you why' and seek to move to argument, but any conclusion will be so value-based (as in, what is 'great' or 'of all time') that it will be impossible to prove.

6.5.1 Glossary

Argument – an attempt to persuade someone to your point of view or conclusion; typically comprises a number of reasons or premises in support of the advocate's claim/conclusion.

Claims – statements or assertions that something is the case; often made without (or before) the production of evidence or proof; can be known facts, forecasts, suggestions, beliefs or opinions and may be true, false, mistaken or lies (e.g. the exit polls suggest that the Conservatives are likely to win an overall majority).

Opinions – judgements or points of view that are subjective by nature (e.g. London is a great city!); an opinion can become an argument when it is supported by facts, but keep in mind that people can draw different opinions from the same facts.

Facts – are verifiable in the sense that they are known or can be proved to be true (e.g. London is the capital of England).

Value judgements – opinions about the value or worth of things (e.g. professional footballers are paid an obscene amount of money).

Evidence – stuff presented in support of an assertion (e.g. my wet hair and raincoat is evidence of my claim that I have been outside in the rain).

Assumptions – things that are believed to be true or certain without the need for proof (e.g. I assume that the lift I get in has been properly serviced and will take me to the 7th floor).

Inference –drawing conclusions from premises known or assumed to be true (e.g. I walk into the house soaking wet and my family infers that it is raining).

6.6 What Are You Arguing?

We touched on this important question in Module A when we looked at the importance of issues. We saw that at some time or another we have all had difficulty guessing what point a speaker is trying to make:

- What's this all about?
- Where is this taking us?
- What's their point?

Judges get particularly annoyed if the direction the advocate's argument is going in is not crystal clear, and will generally call for all points to be enumerated, signposted and clarified (see Chapter 15 Direction). It is only when the direction of travel and an argument's destination are clear that the judge or listener can follow the reasoning process. It therefore makes sense that we should all try and *signpost the direction of our arguments as soon as possible.*

Journalists and lawyers recognise the importance of making the direction of their argument crystal clear within their opening remarks. A skilful *nutshell*, in the form of a headline or opening remark, gives the audience an immediate overview of the argument and the subject matter. Illustration 6.2 is a good example of the process of reduction that Professor Richard Dawkins no doubt had in mind when considering the title of his book.

Illustration 6.2 The God Delusion

Richard Dawkins book, *The God Delusion*, runs to almost 440 pages of polemic argument against the notion of faith. In just three words, his title manages to summarise his point precisely. This is a good example of the skill advocates should develop of succinctly signposting the central thrust of their case or argument in as few words as possible.

6.7 How to Begin?

Lawyers often begin their formal argument by setting out an agenda of what they will be addressing and in what order. The old teaching adage of 'tell them what you are going to tell them, tell them, and then tell them what you've told them', is a sound way to start any presentation. It gives your audience an overview of your submissions and the order you'll be making them in. For example, 'I will argue this evening for the UK's withdrawal from the EU and I shall do so on the basis of three arguments: a, b and c.'

Another way of signposting your argument is to start with a *commonplace* (see Module C for details). This rhetorical device enables you to indicate the nature of your argument and its direction of travel by reference to something that is common knowledge and that is not likely to be contentious. For example, in opening an argument in support of capital punishment the advocate could make his or her position clear: 'Justice demands an eye for an eye and that wrongdoers should pay a price for their wrongs. The price for taking someone's life should be the forfeiture of their own.' (*commonplace* – retribution)

Deciding how to begin is important and the topic is returned to in Chapter 14.

7 • The Reasoning Process

An argument's conclusion can only be as strong as the reasoning that preceded it. Lawyers are always mindful of the rule: weak reasons = weak conclusions.

The stronger and more *concrete* the reasoning, the more persuasive the argument. Consider the following *value judgements* in favour of the death penalty:

- 'Most working people support the death penalty...'
- 'A man jailed for life would have a meaningless existence...'

These premises are weak as they stand and will not provide much underpinning or support for the conclusion. Opponents would counter with:

- 'Do they? How many?'
- 'What evidence can be called upon to support this? Might not some prisoners rehabilitate themselves?'

If an advocate wants to argue along these lines it is best to do research and flesh out their premise with hard *evidence*, such as, 'A survey by ABC in 2013 found that 89% of the working population support capital punishment for child murder.' The makes the argument more compelling because it supports the conclusion by reference to concrete statistical evidence.

Let us consider an example that relates to a reference for Fred: 'Fred worked with me on secondment and I can confirm that he is an excellent and reliable worker.'

The conclusion that 'Fred is an excellent worker' is advanced on a weak premise, that is, 'he worked with me on secondment'. The argument needs to be beefed up.

First, we don't know who has given the reference or whether they have any credibility; it could be Fred's mother! (see Appendix A.3 Ethos). How much experience of employing people does the person have? What is their role within the organisation?

Second, there is no reference as to when Fred worked, what his role was, what he did and for how long.

When planning your argument or assessing your opponents it helps to 'interrogate' them by reference to the six Kipling questions, namely, what, why, when, where, how, and who.

In Fred's case, the reference could be bulked up by recording answers to some of the following questions:

- Who is the person who has given this reference?
- What experience do they have of evaluating people?
- How many other people worked with them at that time?
- How long did Fred work with them?
- What was the nature of their work relationship?
- What did Fred do?
- When was it that they worked together?

When you are seeking to refute or challenge another's argument ask yourself the same types of questions and then emphasise in your argument what is *not said*, for instance: 'My position is that this reference is of little value and should not be relied upon. For example, there is no detail as to the identity of the individual who gave this reference; it could be their mother! Nor is there anything about their work record or status and nothing about their working relationship with Fred. Further, nothing is stated about the nature of Fred's work; what he did, when or for how long. One might imagine that at least some of this information would have been included in the reference had it been available, but we have nothing.'

7.1 Summary

The plausibility and strength of an argument will stand on the strength of its reasoning process. This process can be checked by submitting the reasons to what, why, when, where, how and who questions.

Having identified the importance of the reasoning process and ways in which it can be bench tested, Chapters 8–12 look in more detail at common types of reasoning and the importance of evidence.

8 • Assumptions and Inferences

Understanding how assumptions and inferences work enables us to exploit them as part of our reasoning process, and avoids them becoming a weak link in our arguments. On the other side of the coin, such insights enable us to challenge those who rely on them inappropriately.

Both concepts are dealt with in this chapter because assumptions are often used as the basis for drawing an inference.

8.1 Assumptions

An assumption is something that you 'assume' to be the case. It can be a belief, a prejudice or a conclusion, often reached without the assessment of evidence. Assumptions are not *a bad thing*, they simply reflect our everyday experience of life and help us go about our day-to-day business and to make sense of our world.

Most of the time our assumptions are correct, for instance, that food served in a restaurant will be edible and that airplanes we travel in are well maintained and safe. We'd quickly become paranoid if we weren't able to rely on such assumptions. However, it would be foolish to believe that all assumptions are always correct – sometimes they need testing.

The extent to which we need to test assumptions will reflect the risk inherent in relying on them. So, it makes sense to test our assumptions when the downside of getting it wrong is high, as in the sense of risk of injury or of exposure to contractual penalty. It is no surprise that good project managers take care to test assumptions that have been made when formulating plans.

A simple way of testing an assumption is to apply the *What if?* test:

- *What if* the 'drunk beggar' staggering down the road toward you is neither drunk nor a beggar, but has an illness such as diabetes? How might this questioning have an impact upon your reasoning and actions?
- *What if* the driver at the junction you are approaching is drunk, disqualified and/or reading a smart phone? What difference might that knowledge make to your risk assessment?
- *What if* that important spare part you have ordered does not arrive when promised? Have you any back-up plans?

8.2 Inferences

Inferences often follow assumptions. An inference is a step in your thought process. So, having assumed that the plane we are about to board has been properly serviced we infer that it is safe to proceed. On occasion, we need to be more mindful of this intellectual processing. For example, the process often involves deducing or concluding (something) from evidence and reasoning, rather than from explicit statements. For example, if a colleague in accounts tells you they 'love' your car, this is *direct evidence* of their interest that you can act upon if you choose. However, if the only 'evidence' of their interest is that they have a habit of looking back at your car as they walk across the car park, then you may be none the wiser. However, if your life experience has led you to *assume* that people act in this way if they admire or like something, then you may wish to *infer* that they have an interest in your car sufficient to mention when making small talk at the coffee station.

So, drawing an inference is about making an 'educated guess', of course we may be right or wrong. The issue is to make these educated guesses as smart as possible. The best way of testing an assumption or belief is to revisit it and test how far the evidence supports it. Illustration 8.1 demonstrates this process of revisiting and is a good example of how to analyse an argument based on assumptions and inferences. It is also useful to test assumptions you may have as to your public speaking ability!

Illustration 8.1 Testing assumptions and inferences

I was once asked to coach a colleague who, I was told, was 'petrified' of making presentations because he was 'very poor' at public speaking. I began the coaching session with a focus on the 'issue' of his skill and with a view to testing his assumption.

I began by recognising that he could, of course, be correct in his belief (as to his public speaking ability). However, if such a conclusion could adversely affect his professional life, it would be a good idea to assess how he had reached that viewpoint, that is, review the evidence.

I then explained a little about the way we learn things:

1. We learn from experience. This process is not always straightforward, and some things seem contradictory, and can result in us focusing on some phenomena more than others.

2. Making progress in our learning requires us to formulate assumptions and draw conclusions.

3. On the basis of our assumptions we formulate beliefs that have a great bearing upon how we see things and take action.

My colleague told me that he had always considered himself shy and found it challenging to speak up when the opportunity arose. After school, university and professional training he had formulated the belief that he simply did not have the 'gift of the gab' and had decided that he should avoid occasions when he might be called upon to speak, such as pitches and presentations.

I asked him to objectively assess the 'evidence' of how poor he was at public speaking, and he cited examples of how he had been criticised as a school student at a debate for speaking too fast and using fillers such as 'um' and 'er'. At law school (and mindful of his earlier experience) he was not surprised to be told that he was 'far too fast 'and had to 'slow down'. He had found the feedback process very stressful and had decided that he was beset with anxiety and nerves and was simply not a natural speaker, so he decided to avoid any opportunity to practise his public speaking.

I told him that this was a shame as practising was necessary for learning and developing. I also suggested that the evidence I had heard as to his competence was flimsy – relating as it did to a belief that he was 'shy' and two long-ago, formal assessments when he'd been told he was 'too fast'. I accepted that there might be some validity in that suggestion but that speaking fast was not evidence of being a poor speaker. There were many ways to address this type of problem.

From a learning perspective, my colleague's early feedback experiences had made him conclude that he was evidently poor at public speaking. As a consequence, he had avoided situations where he could challenge that belief by practising and developing his speaking skills. What was needed now was a reappraisal of the 'case' against him (i.e. that he was a poor speaker). He should look at the 'evidence' afresh. How reliable was it? What did it mean? In what context was it given? What assumptions and beliefs resulted from these experiences? How has he fared since these early appraisals, for example, when speaking in smaller groups or was it only large groups that fazed him? Why did he think he went too fast? What could he do to slow down or to create pauses?

What all this resulted in was a fresh enquiry into his strengths and weaknesses: a reappraisal of the evidence. Of course he wasn't a 'poor' speaker; he was simply someone who needed a little help on his pace of delivery and challenging nerves – a relatively easy task.

So, an inference is a conclusion reached on the basis of evidence, reasoning or assumptions. In court a lawyer may invite a judge to infer something, based on the evidence presented. The evidence and submissions must be clear and unambiguous. If they are not, the judge will ask what the lawyer is attempting to establish. It follows that in a court of law there is very little use 'nudge nudge, wink wink' or innuendo in a lawyer's submission.

8.3 Implications

In less formal situations than court you may be invited to draw a conclusion from a state of affairs where the conclusion is not explicitly stated. There is nothing wrong with implying that something is or is not the case, provided that nobody is unduly prejudiced by such a technique. Indeed, there are a host of reasons why we may choose not to be too explicit, for instance, avoiding a spoiler alert when describing a film.

However, we should also have in mind why people are not always explicit, and ensure that they are not seeking to suggest something in a way that is not appropriate. One annoying habit is hinting at something but falling short of spelling it out with a trope such as 'Just saying!' Don't let people get away with suggesting things in this way. Challenge them by asking 'What precisely are you suggesting?' and if they refuse to say what they are hinting at, then cross-examine them by calling them out, for instance, 'Are you suggesting that I stole it?' They will then have to put up or shut up. People often wish to control or bully by speaking in innuendos and insinuations. Be ready to call them out!

9 • Generalisations

*The fundamental cause of the trouble is that
in the modern world the stupid are cocksure
while the intelligent are full of doubt. (Bertrand
Russell, 'The Triumph of Stupidity', 1933)*

A **generalisation is a** conclusion that is often exaggerated and seldom supported by evidence. They can be examples of lazy or sloppy arguments and are easy to shoot down. On the other hand, they can – if skilfully framed and qualified – be extremely engaging and effective during an argument and it is certainly worth thinking about how they work.

Generalisations often relate to one or other of the following:

- Frequency of an event (e.g. a spectrum from always to never)
- Quantity (e.g. from all to none)
- Probability (e.g. from certainly to unlikely).

Examples of generalisations could include:

- Fred is *always* late
- *All* bankers are grossly overpaid
- He will *certainly* get drunk at the party.

The danger with generalisations is that they are often exaggerated, in which case they are easy to refute. To refute the above examples, all one has to do is to cite an example of when the argument/conclusion does not apply, such as, 'That's simply not true, Fred was early on Tuesday' or 'That's not fair, I accept he may get drunk but he doesn't during the day.'

It is always your choice as to how 'high' you decide to pitch an argument and, as we shall see in Module C, it sometimes helps to deliberately exaggerate for effect, and not in the sense of being literal. Of course, everything depends upon context, but assuming that you do not wish to start a 'fight' and/ or simply rile your opponents, it is important to think very carefully about how you frame and qualify a generalisation.

You should want to plant the possibility of something being the case in the mind of your audience in a way that supports your position and influences their decision-making. Generalisations provide a good opportunity to engage with your audience if you take care in choosing appropriate 'qualifiers' to demonstrate precisely what you mean to say.

Return to our three examples (frequency, quantity and probability) and reflect on what words you can use to qualify your meaning (qualifiers are in italics):

- Frequency qualifiers for 'He is always late' – *always, often, sometimes, occasionally, rarely, never*
- Quantity qualifiers for 'All bankers are grossly overpaid' – *all, the majority, many, some, a minority, no*
- Probability qualifiers for 'He will **certainly** get drunk at the party' – *definitely, certainly, probably, may, perhaps, unlikely*.

What the above statements might achieve in an emotive sense can be lost in a rational sense if there is little or no attempt to spell out the evidence or other reasons that support the generalisations. All your opponent has to do is adduce evidence that challenges the generalisation. It follows that, when using a generalisation, it helps to produce examples and evidence that support it – contrast the following generalisations:

1. 'People who own dogs are healthy.'
2. 'Regular exercise is good for you and can keep down weight. For many, a dog is a companion and ensures that an owner goes out for regular exercise. There is also some evidence that having a dog alleviates depression and anxiety. Therefore, people who have a dog are likely to be more healthy than those who do not.'

The first is not supported by any evidence and is put forward in an absolute and unqualified way – 'are healthy'. The second is supported by some evidence and is *qualified* by the words 'are more likely'.

In summary, when generalising be mindful of how your argument can be attacked and make sure you qualify it accordingly.

Illustration 9.1 Mindful arguing

On a political TV programme, the writer and commentator Will Self caused a row in a discussion with a Brexit-supporting MP by seeming to suggest a connection between racism and Brexit supporters. When the MP protested vigorously, Self decided to reframe his point more mindfully, 'What I am suggesting is – probably – that all racists voted Brexit' – an interesting point which could have some merit. In any event, Self managed to reference racism and Brexit in the same sentence.

BBC Politics Live, March 2019

Illustration 9.2 Try this: generalisation

If you want to make a broad statement or generalisation (e.g. all bankers are greedy), try and qualify the proposition and/or concede that there may be exceptions. For example, 'No doubt there are some bankers who think of nothing but the interests of their customers, and give great amounts to charity, but on the whole their remuneration packages point to them being greedy.'

Focus carefully on precisely what you wish to emphasise, as the qualifier will point to what you want people to consider. For instance, 'I'm not saying that Fred is **always** late, indeed I remember one occasion last year when he arrived at his desk before I got in, but I don't think that he himself would say he was an early bird, and perhaps he would concede that he is late more often than he is on time.'

If attacking someone else's use of a generalisation, such as 'Kids have it tough nowadays', use exceptions to demonstrate that the generality and width of the proposition renders it unreliable.

10 • Evidence

A **persuasive argument is** built on a solid foundation of evidence.

Evidence is information that proves something. Generally, evidence is only required to prove facts that are disputed between the parties. It can take several forms, including: *documents*, such as contracts, photographs or charts; *physical objects*, such as a gun or DNA; or *witness testimonies*, such as oral or written statements.

The best evidence is strong evidence that is authoritative and relevant. This chapter looks at how to distinguish strong evidence from weak evidence.

10.1 The Advocate Giving Evidence

Advocates are more credible if they are deemed to have no personal interest in the outcome of the argument. In a courtroom their function is to present their client's arguments and to adduce evidence that supports those arguments. They do not give evidence themselves.

The best persuasive evidence is independent. In a practical sense, this means that if you are planning to present an argument – perhaps at a negotiation – you should concentrate on other people's accounts and not find yourself giving evidence (e.g. 'I can recall precisely what I said on that occasion and I certainly did not agree to increasing the fee.')

If your evidence is crucial to the outcome of the argument then it is best to get someone else to present the case for you.

Take note of ancient advice, often misattributed to Abraham Lincoln, 'He who represents himself has a fool for a client.'

10.2 Reliability of Sources

The weight of an argument correlates with the reliability of the evidential sources. For example, if debating global warming, arguments will have greater clout if the evidence can be attributed to an authority, such as an academic. Contrast, 'Global warming has been recognised as a problem for ages' with 'Global warming was first recognised as an issue by Wallace Smith Broecker of Columbia University in a seminal report of 1975.'

The practical application of this note is that when you present a third-party account you should think about what aspects of their background to include for additional clout. For example, 'Mrs. Brady's recollection of what was agreed at the lunch is radically different from the claimants. Mrs. Brady is an experienced businesswoman who, apart from running this property business, is a marketing consultant and sits as a magistrate. In light of this I invite you to infer that she is an individual with excellent recall and professionalism and that her recollection can be relied upon.'

The advocate should be presenting the evidence given by Mrs Brady, perhaps in a statement that includes details of her professional standing. If her statement did not include these details, then the advocate would not be able to make such references, as to do so would constitute giving evidence, which as we have seen is not generally permitted.

10.3 Neutral and Impartial Accounts

Just as a shopper might not be totally persuaded by a pushy salesperson telling them that a tight-fitting suit is a 'great fit', an audience will not necessarily attach great weight to evidence from those with an interest in the outcome. It follows that the evidence of an interested party should be corroborated if at all possible.

Scrutinise your opponent's evidence to see whether a witness has any bias and/or interest in the outcome. If they do then seek to downplay the importance of their contribution.

10.4 Hearsay

Hearsay is evidence that is based on information received from another. So, if John says that he knows Peter has stolen his wallet because Susan told him she saw him take it, John's evidence (certainly in a criminal court) is not admissible. Susan is the one who can give a credible account.

Illustration 10.1 Levels of evidence

If Joan wants to establish that she is a reliable worker a reference from a past employer will carry more clout than a note from her husband.

If Joan wants to demonstrate that she loves her husband her claim that she tells him this every morning proves very little.

If Frank wants to establish that he made a booking at a restaurant for a window table at 8.30pm, shouting this at the receptionist will not prove very much. He should consider what the restaurant might concede. If they concede that Frank rang to book a table last Tuesday morning, that is a good start. If they accept that his booking was for 8.30 that too is good. If the head waiter then acknowledges that

Frank always sits at the window seat then Frank is getting somewhere. The point of this is that Frank is building his case on the concessions (evidence) he is extracting from the restaurant not simply by repeating himself over and over.

If Susan wants to establish that she purchased an article from Marks and Spencer on 10 June 2017 then a receipt will help, as written supporting evidence is generally very persuasive. But this is not always the case and the evidential weight will depend upon who produced the evidence. For example, if Susan wants to show that she arranged for the plumber to come to her house on Tuesday, her diary note will not in itself establish that this was agreed.

11 • Cause and Effect

'Nothing comes from nothing'
Lucretius, De Rerum Notura

Module A looked at 'What happened?', which is often considered alongside 'Why did it happen?', which involves a careful reflection on cause and effect. Lawyers are particularly concerned with *causation*, as it is often necessary to show a connection between one party's act or omission and the consequences suffered by another party.

Cause and effect arguments happen daily, often without any real thought or analysis. For example, 'Mary was running too fast (*cause*) and as a consequence fell over (*effect*)'. But what if: her shoes had high heels; she'd spent the afternoon in the pub; or she was running over a badly maintained pavement?

Always bear in mind that, more often than not, many causes contribute to an event and a nuanced argument reflects the possibilities. This qualification is often forgotten and people rush to argue a cause that suits their own agenda. For example, a binary argument ensues whenever there is another terrible shooting incident in the USA. The gun lobby rush to blame 'mental health', while advocates of gun control argue that poor gun control is the main cause. The reality is that they are both correct to some extent as both mental health and gun control are contributing causes.

If we wish to advance sophisticated arguments, we should acknowledge these complexities and seek to evidence why the cause that we are focusing on is the predominant or more probable one. It is often sensible to make a strategic concession to facilitate your focus.

Illustration 11.1 Sophisticated arguments

'We should discourage use of soft drugs as they lead on to more dangerous drugs, such as heroin'.

The shortcoming with such arguments is that they are open to challenge on the basis that there are many reasons why 'things happen'. Therefore, it helps if you can beef up your **cause and effect** argument with evidence and examples, that support the sense of your explanation (see Appendix A.5 Logos)

The above example would become: 'It is extremely likely that those who use heroin have at some time used cannabis. Cannabis is an illegal drug and its use constitutes a criminal offence. One can imagine exposure to a criminal fraternity who have no scruples and try to sell you anything that makes them a return. Trading in heroin is very profitable...'

Illustration 11.2 Try this: cause and effect

When advancing a cause and effect argument, such as having a dog as a pet makes people more healthy, make sure you ask yourself **why** that is the case. Be prepared to list the reasons, for instance: people who have dogs have to exercise them; walking is good for health; dogs are good companions and help relieve the symptoms of loneliness; and so on.

---

12 • Theory of Case and the Role of Stories

Anyone responsible for investigating a situation can be overwhelmed by the sheer volume of incoming information. Management consultants, teachers, start-up entrepreneurs, police officers, and even lawyers, need to manage the influx by sorting, classifying, organising and, most importantly, simplifying the information in a manner that lends itself to the persuasive presentation of findings. It will certainly not suffice to uncritically dump all the unearthed information and facts on your target audience to 'please make of this what you will'. It is the advocate's responsibility to present a plausible explanation, whether as a recommendation, an investment proposal, an indictment or a submission to a jury. Lawyers refer to this as a 'theory of case'.

The daunting amount of material can raise a multitude of issues. Many of the witness statements, expert reports and relevant documents will be conflicting, but they all need to be considered and then woven into the advocate's theory of case. Most lawyers begin working on their theory of case as early as possible to build a working hypothesis they can modify as the case develops.

A sensible theory of case considers both strengths and weaknesses, and any shortcomings must be identified and addressed. For example, inconsistencies and differences in recollections in witness accounts need to be explained. Documentary evidence (e.g. emails or notes) may contradict a recollection and/or there are problems with the credibility of a witness (e.g. their motive). An ignored weakness could impact the credibility of your whole case. How you deal with them will depend upon the context, but it is sensible to remain positive and not be too fazed, as undue concern will not help your cause. Hopefully, you'll have more strengths than weaknesses! Remember, if you can't deal with a weakness it is best to acknowledge that and focus on your strengths.

As we saw in Chapter 2, facts will underpin our arguments and they play a key role in a theory of case. At an early stage, a lawyer develops a factual narrative and chronology to deal with what happened before, during and after the events being considered.

As the matter moves towards a negotiation or trial, the lawyer reviews the evidence and begins to develop and rehearse a number of evidence-based arguments. Although each argument may be reasoned, clear and easy to follow, there will be strands that address different issues which do not necessarily 'hang' together well in the theory of case. Then you need to develop the arguments into a coherent group so that they all flow in the same direction to support and build the theory of case.

At the same time, lawyer's work hard to precis the theory of case and to summarise in a few sentences precisely what the case is and why it is likely to succeed (see Chapter 15 Direction).

It is not easy to iron out inconsistencies and to reduce the arguments to their essence. A lawyer spends much time rehearsing precisely how the case will best be presented at the negotiation or trial.

One way to present the threads of an argument in an organised, coherent and effortless form is to present the theory of case as a story. The importance of storytelling is returned to in Chapter 19. Illustration 12.1 describes the transformational power of stories.

Illustration 12.1 Try this: storytelling

'When we have made an experience or a chaos into a story we have transformed it, made sense of it, transmuted experience, domesticated the chaos.' (from Ben Okri's *Birds of Heaven*)

Ben Okri believes that stories can transform our understanding of a narrative and they are a central theme in his book, *Birds of Heaven*. The 'experience' and 'chaos' he refers to can be thought of as the preparation that we undertake on the theory of case in preparation for a negotiation or hearing. During this preparation a lawyer hopes for a transformative insight that enables them to see the 'story'. At this point of 'enlightenment' everything becomes crystal clear. Such a transformational moment is explained in Illustration 12.3.

Okri suggests that stories enable people to make sense of things and to see things that they've not seen before. He says that great religions and cultures are stories easily understood and learnt, which enable them to be passed between generations.

The insight for a coherent theory of case can coincide with the lawyer identifying the DNA of the case. By recognising how the case hangs together, an advocate can express their theory of case in a few words, that is, why they are going to win. In commercial scenarios these outcomes are sometimes referred to as 'straplines'.

Illustration 12.2 Straplines

Marketing people look for **straplines** that reflect their organisation's culture and values, so as encapsulate their offering – or argument.

> For example: the 'Take Back Control' slogan is felt to have appealed to voters in the 2016 Brexit election; mention has already been made of the title for Richard Dawkins's *The God Delusion* – three words that summarise the detailed arguments he makes in his book.

The references in Illustration 12.1 are well-known examples of reducing an argument to its essence. It is certainly a quality seen in leaders and good speakers, which manifests in many ways. For example, after listening carefully to a detailed discussion a good advocate can summarise in a sentence or two the central thrust of the argument or position. They can articulate the essence of their theory of case. They have developed the skill of synthesising, which enables them to pull different strands together and to report them in a way that advances a central point or hypothesis.

Central to all these skills is the ability to conceive of and tell a good story.

Stories enable people to see things differently. They provide an explanation based on evidence that the audience has encountered. They make sense. Of course, before an advocate can persuade anyone of their story (argument) they must first see it themselves.

Imagine that there is to be a trial to determine whether Illustration 12.3 is an image is of an old or a young woman. Do you feel confident that you could argue both sides? It is probable that one side of the argument appeals immediately, which can make it hard to see the other side.

Although the arguments are radically different, they are based on the same evidence, the image. The successful advocate will be the one who not only sees their case clearly, but is also able to flesh out their explanation in a convincing and plausible way. This will involve some creative setting of the scene, a skill that comes more easily to creative people, such as storytellers.

Illustration 12.3 Exercise: image of a lady

© Wikimedia Commons/W.E. Hill

The importance of storytelling is returned to in Chapter 19 when two competing stories for the image of a lady are suggested.

Module C
Presenting an Argument and the Role of Advocacy

13 • Advocacy

Time spent in finding out what has happened and then devising a response is wasted if the outcome of that process, in the form of an argument or strategy, is neither advanced nor implemented.

For a lawyer, this generally means trying to negotiate a favourable settlement or preparing a case for trial. The lawyer's role is to represent and argue their client's case, fearlessly and independently. This process is one example of advocacy, but advocacy is not only done by lawyers. Anyone entrusted with advancing and/or arguing a cause or a policy is an advocate, which is how this term is used throughout Module C.

Why, when and how a non-lawyer presents their arguments depends upon the type of argument and their responsibility for its advancement. This is a good place to re-emphasise the central role of argument in almost everything we do. For example, an argument might involve a one-off, straightforward exercise such as asking someone to take their feet off a train seat, or a worker asking their boss for a wage increase. These straightforward examples have involved some degree of assessment, preparation and execution. On other occasions, argument involves more complex interactions, such as formulating and articulating policies, campaigns and strategies, such as: launching an advertising campaign; formulating a policy to increase diversity in the police force; or devising a strategy to increase share in a particular market.

In any of these situations – whether straightforward or complex – the person responsible for selling the outcome must move from a predominately reflective stage (assessment and reasoning), to an active stage in which they advocate their argument for the benefit of themselves or others.

Module C addresses how an advocate can present a winning argument – and the qualities described can apply to any advocate, in any argument. The scope of this module is shown by the emphasised terms in Illustration 13.1.

Illustration 13.1 Contents of Module C

A winning argument has **clarity** and is put forward by a **resilient** advocate **confidentially** and **enthusiastically**. Such an argument is likely to reflect an understanding of the rhetorical trope, the **three pillars of persuasion**, by showing the advocate's **credibility (ethos)** and containing an appeal to the audience's **reason (logos)** and **emotions (pathos)**. The argument will be properly **reasoned** and **structured** and delivered in a way that demonstrates an understanding of different types of **rhetorical mode**. It will be **framed** and presented in an **engaging** way by a credible advocate.

A lawyer will understand that building **engagement** and **rapport** is aided by making a **good first impression**. Being **well prepared** and having a grasp of **key rhetorical techniques** will make arguments more compelling, as will the **clarity** of the argument.

An advocate's persuasive skills are used in negotiation to settle disputes without going to trial. The strength of someone's hand at a negotiation will depend upon the strength of their **evidence**, the way it is **organised** and **structured** as strong arguments contained in a compelling **case theory**. An advocate knows that an argument is only as strong as its **evidential weakest link**, and its prospect of success will be enhanced if it can be described in **story** format.

As Illustration 13.1 makes it apparent, rhetoric – defined as the art of persuasion – is an integral and important part of advocacy. It follows that an understanding of some of its key principles and techniques is important for those who wish to improve their persuasive skills.

If you'd like to study these rhetorical ideas in 'one sitting' see Appendix A, which begins with a note on why rhetoric is important and then addresses seven important aspects. Alternatively, you can refer to the appropriate sections of Appendix A as the topic is referred to in the main body of the book.

The topics relevant to winning an argument are set out in the following six chapters, each of which focuses on an important element of advocacy. To help your understanding and to encourage critical assessment each chapter includes a table on the *behavioural evidence of competence*. These tables illustrate how the issues discussed in the chapter can be evidenced by reference to behaviour, described as either *competent* or *not competent*. The analyses provide a good reference for advocates who wish to reflect upon their own aptitude and/or development. These behavioural matrixes can also provide concrete feedback for training or coaching.

14 • Audacity

Courage is rightly esteemed the first of human qualities, because, as has been said, it is the quality which guarantees all others. (Winston Churchill, Collier's magazine, 1931)

How **often do** people leave a meeting or finish a telephone conversation and then agonise over what they *should* have said? Resolving to do things differently next time is rarely sufficient to bring about a desired change in behaviour. To make a real difference requires not only a resolution, but also an understanding of *how* to do things differently and an awareness of *what* needs to be changed. This reflective process lies at the heart of experiential learning.

To achieve our goals and ambitions – whether they be long-term career or strategic goals, or short-term objectives – we must be assertive and prepared to push the boundaries. Lawyers are trained to do this. As advocates or spokespersons for their clients they must feel 100% confident that they are presenting the best argument possible. Much of what they argue will reflect their client's instructions and they should never be apologetic in presenting their client's case to a third party. If they feel a client has a bad point, they should advise them of this and question the wisdom of making a specific submission. However, if the client still instructs that those arguments should be put, then it is the lawyer's job to advance them with conviction. A lawyer's task is to be assertive – and we will look at precisely what that means later – for now, let's consider how being assertive can change things not only for ourselves but also for others.

Illustration 14.1 Advocacy watch: Rosa Parks

In 1955 Rosa Parks was neither a political activist nor an experienced advocate but when she was asked to give up her bus seat for a white person she decided she'd had enough of racism and decided to speak out, 'I don't think I should have to stand up.'

Rosa later said, 'I did not want to be mistreated, I did not want to be deprived of a seat that I had paid for. It was just time ... there was opportunity for me to take a stand to express the way I felt about being treated in that manner. I had not planned to get arrested. I had plenty to do without having to end up in jail. But when I had to face that decision, I didn't hesitate to do so because I felt that we had endured that too long. The more we gave in, the more we complied with that kind of treatment, the more oppressive it became.' (from a 1992 National Public Radio interview about the bus boycott)

14.1 Confidence and Conviction

Bad advocates often appear to lack not only confidence but also any enthusiasm for the argument they are making – as if they can't be bothered. Or they are defensive or apologetic, as in, 'Don't shoot the messenger'. Clearly, an advocate who is not persuaded by the credibility of their own argument is unlikely to persuade others.

It is the advocate's job to engage with and enthuse their audience. They may be arguing on behalf of somebody they dislike, or putting forward a point of view they believe has little prospect of success. Nevertheless, in each case they should assume responsibility and argue with conviction and confidence.

Illustration 14.2 Arguing with confidence and conviction

I was mentoring a young lawyer who was preparing for his first contested court trial. During the preparation he met with the client and went through the issues that would have to be determined by the court. One of the contested points – relating to whether a contract term was ratified – was very weak and almost bound to fail. Accordingly, the lawyer sensibly advised the client that it was best to concede the ratification point and focus on the strong parts of their case. This was good advice, as there was little point distracting the court with an argument that was almost bound to fail; it was much better to focus on stronger points. However, the client refused to accept the advice and said that, for commercial reasons, he was not happy to abandon the ratification point. The advocate was in a situation where he had been instructed to argue a point that he was convinced had little prospect of success. He asked me for advice and I told him that he should be very careful not to sound apologetic or defeatist when he argued that point. If he showed that he felt the point had little merit, then he was bound to lose it. Instead, he should look the court in the eye and make the point with enthusiasm and determination. He won the case – and succeeded on the ratification point!

Having 100% confidence in the integrity of your argument is not the same as being 100% confident of winning. It simply means that the argument is the best argument you can advance in the circumstances. An advocate who has that confidence will make a more persuasive and engaging case.

Above all, an audacious advocate does not give up. They understand that their argument is more likely to succeed at some times than at others. Such an advocate may concede that they have lost a battle, but not the war – which brings us nicely to one of history's most determined and pugnacious advocates.

Illustration 14.3 Advocacy watch: Was Churchill persuasive?

History suggests that even the great man lacked persuasive appeal from time to time. For example, he had difficulty winning over the appeasers prior to 1939 and he spent many years trying to persuade the House of Commons about the risk Hitler posed. He had a similar failure when he lost the general election in 1945, when his credibility was not as compelling as during the war years.

From this, we can deduce that the timing of an argument is crucial to its prospect of success. Advocates have to bear this in mind when planning their strategy and advising those they represent.

Rhetorical reference: kairos (timing), the ability to make the right argument at the right time. This notion reflects the fact that argument and rhetoric have to be looked at in the context of time. Is this the right moment to run this line of argument or to make this application or to give this speech?

Being candid is an attractive quality and one should never try to hide or cover up the weakness of one's position. Related to this is that it is generally better to deliver bad news on your own terms rather than to let your opponent milk it to their own advantage (see Concede points in Chapters 18.1 and 20.7).

14.2 Taking a View

A confident advocate quickly tires of sitting on the fence, and is not afraid or slow to 'take a view'.

However, showing your hand or taking up a position takes courage. It often means entering into an adversarial dynamic, where you have to defend your position and/or attack other's.

Bear in mind that your argument is as valid as anyone else's and that you are as entitled to your point of view as the next person. Arguing with enthusiasm and commitment ensures that you impact the debate and most people will treat your contribution with respect.

Of course, people will point to what they consider are shortcomings and flaws in your argument – and it is often wise to note such contributions. Always have in mind that, as the advocate, you are responsibile for making the argument. Don't let *perfect be the enemy of good* and remember that there is no such thing as a flawless argument; if there were, there would be no need to debate or seek resolution. It helps to imagine how successful entrepreneurs have persuaded people to their point of view through resilience and determination. Love them or loathe them, they all share an infectious enthusiasm that helps them build an impressive ethos and pathos appeal (see Appendices A.3–4).

Illustration 14.4 Growing confidence

A young student I was coaching was preparing for a debate on whether private education should be banned. His position was that it should be, and he shared with me a number of compelling arguments he proposed making. I asked what his problem was, and he said it was about presenting in a confident manner. He'd been asked what he was debating by some family friends and had been met with a barrage of negative responses. As a result, he was beginning to get cold feet and lose confidence that he could build a compelling case. I advised him that when next asked he should not only say what the debate was about, but also volunteer a brief precis of what his main points were. For example, 'I'll be arguing that the continuation of private education is wrong as, in a meritocracy, the role of education should be to create equal rights and opportunities for all, not just the wealthy, and that bringing all children into the state system would improve the standards of all our schools across the board.'

I told him that getting his points across first was akin to getting in the first punch and it put the opposition on the defensive. He acted on my advice and said that starting like that helped his confidence grow. He became aware that by starting confidently the listener would invariably **have** to deal with his arguments first, before going on to their points. Having your arguments addressed is far better than not getting your arguments across for fear of rejection.

The individualism of advocacy applies to both the argument and the way it is presented. No committee could devise a winning argument and/or a way of presenting it, they'd come up with a compromise – or fudge. Trust your instincts and always remember Winston Churchill's advice that 'perfection spells paralysis'.

14.3 Assertiveness

For the sake of simplicity let's assume that personal behavioural traits can be divided into two broad types: aggressive and submissive. This is a crude characterisation but I hope that the following examples demonstrate the divide.

14.3.1 Aggressive: me, me, me

It is important when considering *audacity* to distinguish and separate out aggressive behaviour. It comes in many forms but almost always involves putting the rights and interests of the aggressive individual above those of any third party. Behaviour can range from *direct* (e.g. a punch on the nose) to *passive* (e.g. a rude verbal put-down or an out-of-hand rejection).

People can also display passive-aggressive behaviour when expressing disapproval or bad feeling toward others in an indirect manner that suggests a degree of negativity. For example, the use of sarcasm or of negative body language such as folded arms.

Aggressive behaviour rides roughshod over other's feelings and attitudes. It is the antithesis of engaging behaviour – an engaging advocate talks *to* their audience, an aggressive advocate talks *at* them. Such an approach is disrespectful and can alienate third parties and cause them distress or fright.

Finally, aggressive behaviour is lazy and counterproductive. Although bullies can gain a short-term benefit, aggressive behaviour rarely reaps dividends in the longer term. I strongly advise against it becoming your default mode.

14.3.2 Submissive: you, you, you

If aggressive behaviour is about 'fighting' then submissive behaviour is about taking 'flight', 'bottling it', or at least trying to avoid an unpleasant confrontation. This is compounded by a lack of resilience.

Most of us dislike confrontation and prefer to avoid it. There is nothing wrong with this provided that, as a consequence, you do not put other people's interests before your own. If you find yourself apologising for something you know you need not apologise for, or feel you make too many concessions when none are required, then perhaps you could benefit from adopting a more assertive style. It certainly helps to bear in mind that argument need not be confrontational. Instead, think of it as a discussion leading to an agreement, that is, a negotiation which tests assumptions, conclusions, criticisms, arguments and decisions.

14.4 Assertive Behaviour

To assert simply means to state a fact or belief confidently and forcefully.

All advocates should have well-developed assertive skills to deal with a crunch point, perhaps in a negotiation, or when making a complaint.

Many people find it difficult or challenging to be assertive and fear rejection. For example: when trying to organise a 'busy' tradesman you spend too long discussing their logistical difficulties at the expense of considering your own. In other situations, such as a negotiation, people are often uncomfortable or find it difficult to put forward a proposition or to make an opening offer.

Being assertive is not a natural human behaviour. Generally, we are hostage to our emotions and switch between anger and fear, depending upon the circumstances. For example, if we see a dog owner allowing his pet to foul the street our ability/desire to remonstrate may be influenced by how confident we feel that our intervention will result in a positive outcome.

Understanding assertive behaviour enables us to focus on our own behaviour and adapt it to meet our objectives. A good way of improving your assertive skills is by modelling your behaviour on someone you feel has these skills. Leaders and bosses are often assertive and you can see at first-hand how they get things done and tackle difficulties. Certainly, these insights can be of great benefit in the workplace, where it is often necessary to assert confidently and without fear.

Assertive behaviour cannot be learnt overnight. The key is to practise.

14.5 Developing Assertive Behaviour

It is not easy to become more assertive. The first thing to do is to recognise why you wish to be more assertive and on which occasions you can practise these skills. The next thing is to believe that improvements can be made and to understand that, as is often the case, preparation is central.

Illustration 14.5 Developing assertive behaviour

I worked with Fred, a young qualified lawyer who felt that he was weak on face-to-face interventions. He'd concluded that he was more cut out for a back-room role, and didn't aspire to heading-up deals and negotiations.

I accepted that Fred might be correct, but that it was perhaps a little too early to decide on exactly how his career would pan out.

Fred confided that he wanted to be more like his boss. I suggested that he should work on his assertiveness and use his boss as a role model.

One thing that he particularly liked about his boss's approach was his use of the phone. If anything needed working out or a problem needed addressing, his boss would simply pick up the phone and speak to the other side. Fred confided that he disliked making calls and that he preferred to correspond by email. He would negotiate contract points by email, then notice that things were becoming protracted and ask his boss to help. The boss would invariably pick up the phone and resolve the problem.

I asked Fred to reflect on why he was uncomfortable about telephoning. He confided that he treated any rejection of his proposals as a personal slight. It seemed that he was unable to separate out a rejection of his proposal from a rejection of himself. I asked him to reflect on how professional courtroom advocates have to assert all manner of things on behalf of their clients and needed to argue independently and without fear of rejection. Recognising that the advocate was independent of the argument was key to accepting that a rejection of your position was not a personal rebuke.

I told Fred that the sooner he got used to talking difficult issues through with the other side, the sooner he would begin to behave like his boss. Of course, there would be calls that he would not find easy and he would often have to deal with aggressive people, but that he should remember that the aggression was the other party's problem, not his, and that there were techniques he could use on such occasions.

For example, I told him that to prepare for the call he should anticipate the answers he feared and then write down some responses, such as, 'What do you mean "no way"?' and 'How do you suggest that we deal with my client's position?'

By practising putting the ball back in the other's court he would build his confidence and test the strength of the other's position.

Finally, I asked Fred to look at research that shows our expectations of responses are often wrong. In particular, it has shown that those who fear rejection are often pleasantly surprised and that 'yes' is a more frequent outcome than we dared hope.

The following highlights the main steps to developing your assertiveness.

- Make sure you are completely prepared and have a firm grasp of the background facts. Preparing in this way increases your confidence and enables you to answer questions. Knowing the details of a case also enables you to ask questions, which can defuse aggression.
- As part of your preparation reflect on how people are likely to behave and think of strategies to respond. For example, if you believe someone is likely to be verbally abusive or sexist, it is best to have prepared

responses and to have practised them. Your practice and preparation will make you feel more in control and more confident that you'll be able to handle the situation.

- Always believe you will succeed. People who are naturally aggressive often only have one gear, and they are put off their stride by people who remain calm and focused and do not respond with similar aggression.

Illustration 14.6 Mediation

I was once asked to mediate an insurance claim for which the claimants had instructed a very aggressive New York lawyer to represent them. I was told that the attorney would bluster and bully and appear completely reluctant to move or concede during the negotiations. I decided beforehand that I would remain calm and not appear put off by any aggression. The rude attorney arrived and, having identified that I was the mediator, he said, 'I'm very busy and I don't want to waste my time, so it is important that you understand that we are not leaving here with a penny less than $750,000. Here, let me write that down for you.' He wrote the figure on my notepaper and turned away. My response could have been, 'Thank you for that. It is helpful to know your position at this time.' What I did say was, 'So you won't settle for $749,999?' The lawyer turned around and said, 'Don't bullshit me!'

The case was settled for about $400,000.

Illustration 14.7 Try This: developing assertive skills

Devise a number of scenarios in which you can practise being assertive.

1. Calling a popular restaurant to make a reservation when you know from experience that they likely to be fully booked. Don't begin: 'I'm wondering whether you may be able to fit us in on Saturday – I know it's a busy night – but.' Instead try,

'Good evening. I'd like to book a table for four on Saturday evening at 7.30 please.' You're still likely to hear, 'I'm very sorry, we are fully booked at that time.' But the way in which you have asked the question will make the listener feel obliged to look and see if anything can be done.

2. When booking a venue for a course I was left wondering whether the price I'd been quoted included tea and coffee for the delegates. I asked them to 'Please confirm that the price includes tea and coffee', rather than asking 'Does the price include tea and coffee?' Can you see how the way a question is put can make a difference to the answer?

Practice asking for things that you would not normally expect, such as an upgrade on an airplane, a window seat in a restaurant, a discount in a shop. Practice complaining more often. Study the responses you get and begin to believe that asking for what you want often yields rewards.

Of course, many inexperienced (and experienced) advocates will get very nervous and there is a section on managing anxiety and nerves in Appendix B.6.

14.6 Rhetorical Underpinning

Much of this chapter has addressed the advocate's credibility. An audacious advocate has a strong *ethos* appeal and understands how rhetorical modes help to differentiate strands of an argument. For example, flagging up explanatory content can help head off a premature attempt to rebuke (see Appendix A.5)

Table 14.1 Behavioural evidence of competence: audacity

Audacity qualities	Competent	Not competent
The advocate takes ownership, prepares properly, accepts responsibility and acts fearlessly and independently The advocate is resilient and argues with tenacity, self-confidence and courage	• Confidently takes control • Sets out clear and unequivocal agendas/arguments • Is independent, takes full responsibility and does not blame others • Creates good ethos appeal • Not distracted by nerves • Deals head-on with difficulties and shortcomings in argument • Understands rhetorical modes and when it is not necessary to argue • Is prepared to make concessions and admit mistakes • Has 100% confidence in argument advanced • Assertive (see separate Table 14.2) • Argues enthusiastically • Strong oratorical skills	• Is a messenger (e.g. 'I am instructed to suggest that...') • Equivocal • Apologetic • Poor eye contact • Negative body language • Afraid of losing • Arrogant

Table 14.2 Behavioural evidence of competence: assertiveness

Assertiveness qualities	Competent	Not competent
The advocate takes ownership of what is said and is honest, direct and unapologetic The advocate treats others and their views with respect The advocate argues with tenacity, self-confidence and courage	• Comfortable and confident • Able to seek help or assistance from others • Not troubled by saying 'no' • At ease speaking to those in authority, such as employers • Not put off by emotional content • Does not blame others	• Submissive and fearful of failure • Does not take ownership • Attacks other people and their views • Apologetic • Poor eye contact • Negative body language • Arrogance

15 • Direction

Flagging up the direction of an argument and condensing its *content* to its core will be appreciated by most audiences. *An audience should never have to ask any of the following questions:*

- What's this all about?
- Where is this going?
- What's the speaker's point?

15.1 First Impressions

Journalists and professional advocates recognise the importance of making the direction of their argument clear from the outset. A skilful *nutshell* gives an audience an immediate overview of the argument and its subject matter.

Having in mind a clear precis of the argument enables an advocate to make an immediate impact and to start confidently. If you write down your opening comments and rehearse them you'll feel confident of a strong start to your advocacy.

Illustration 15.1 Rhetorical technique: hypophora

Hypophora is to pose a rhetorical question (a very engaging tactic in itself) and then to answer it. It's a great technique for starting a verbal presentation that simultaneously engages your audience and signposts your argument.

For example: 'Should we allow fracking? I would say that for the sake of our environment and our economy we should not.'

The *primacy/recency effect* suggests that at the start of a presentation our short-term memory is less crowded and that, as a consequence, what is said at the outset is likely to have a greater impact upon the audience than subsequent comments. An advocate should have this in mind when planning opening remarks. *Recency* relates to the fact that people tend to remember the points made at the end of a sequence – so a strong finish is also advisable.

15.2 Vision and Direction

Spelling out the direction of travel at the outset enables an advocate to signal the nature of the submissions to come. However, a radical vision or proposition may evoke an initial negative response from an audience (watch out for raised eyebrows), who then focus more on the obstacles than the suggested outcomes. Although the obstacles need to be addressed, they can be attended to when the advocate chooses. It follows that, at the outset, the advocate should keep their argument directed toward the end-game and should not be distracted, for 'obstacles… are what you see when you take your eyes off your goals' (attributed to Henry Ford).

A good argument, advanced passionately and with a view to the future can change the course of history. But these types of arguments generally require audacity, as demonstrated in Illustration 15.2.

Illustration 15.2: 'I have a dream'

Martin Luther King's great speech, delivered from the steps of the Lincoln Memorial in Washington DC on 28 August 1963, is a rhetorical masterpiece. No viewing of this great speech is ever a waste of time. A few pointers to watch out for are:

1. Ethos appeal: the speech is in the style of a sermon and is biblical in its resonance and references. Note his reference to 'five score years ago' – what was his inspiration for this phrase?

2. Tense: he uses both demonstrative and deliberative tones as he appeals to values and to a future vision.

3. Anaphora: the repetition of a phrase at the beginning of a sentence is a compelling rhetorical device that can be used in many situations.

Great advocates create a vision, articulate the vision, passionately own the vision and relentlessly drive it forward to completion. Their direction of travel is always clear.

15.2.1 Sense of collaboration

The position advanced must appeal to the audience. Good advocates are skilled in describing their positions to illuminate the attractiveness of the argument and/or to identify shared benefits. To do so, the advocate must truly understand what drives their audience and how they can frame their presentation to capitalise on this knowledge.

15.2.2 Sense of purpose

An audience should seldom have to ask an advocate to explain where a line of argument is going. It should be crystal clear – unless the advocate deliberately decides to hold back information or encourages the audience to guess what the point is.

Alternatively, an advocate may wish to draw attention to something by pretending to gloss over it (e.g. 'I am not suggesting that the person was drunk.'). This kind of irony is referred to as *paralipsis* and it can be used to good effect in a number of advocacy situations.

Direction is about asking yourself what your arguments/ goals are and then identifying carefully what obstacles need to be addressed. An advocate will always be clear about what issues are to be addressed and this understanding is central to both preparation and delivery (see Chapter 17 Clarity). Prepare a chronology of events and build this into your skeleton argument, which will form a 'route planner' that can be referred to as arguments are delivered.

15.2.3 Change of tense

One way of identifying what the key issues are likely to be is to reflect on why there is a need for an argument in the first place. Issues can often be identified by considering tense (see Appendix A.7):

1. **Blame** – relating to things that have already happened and that require a forensic or judicial approach (e.g. Who was responsible for the accident?)
2. **Values** – relating to an assessment of what is 'right' or 'wrong' (e.g. How much fine should be levied?)
3. **Choice** – relating to what we are going to do in the future (e.g. How should we reform the economy?)

The importance of these distinctions lies in the fact that an advocate will not progress to their goals if they get embroiled in the wrong type of argument (tense). Strategically switching tense can move an argument on in your favour.

Table 15.1 Behavioural evidence of competence: direction

Direction qualities	Competent	Not competent
The advocate, through a process of preparation and judgement, is able to summarise a pointed and coherent argument	• Argument(s) clearly signposted and focused toward identifiable objectives • Understands the technical context (e.g. any legal test and/or burden) that must be addressed • Knows precisely what the issues are that form the basis of the argument • Has a strong grasp of the facts and knows which are agreed and which are contested • Prepares well, as evidenced by clear structure, theme, skeleton and aids • Carefully chosen words and themes • Coherent with emphasis and not frightened to make concessions	• Divergent • Winging it • Too many points • Lack of focus and/or consistency (e.g. on description of parties) • Ambiguity and/or inconsistency • Poor or sloppy use of language

Table 15.2 Behavioural evidence of competence: vision

Vision qualities	Competent	Not competent
The explanation the advocate has in mind and that will enable them to achieve their objectives	• A leader • Confident and original thinker • Prepares extremely well and knows how each aspect of the evidence 'fits' with the case • Invites the audience to draw inferences from the evidence • Is able to describe how each part of the evidence fits in • Suggests motives and explanations that can be inferred • Creative mindset	• Winging it • Incoherent • A follower • Discounts the vagaries of people • Takes a too rational approach to the case analysis • Does not understand the structure of a story

16 • Organisation

Advocates often find it difficult to know where to begin and, as a consequence, can conflate their arguments, evidence and issues. Although the destination of the argument may be clear, deciding on the precise route may present challenges. René Descartes, the French philosopher, has some good practical advice on how to begin planning.

Illustration 16.1 René Descartes on the importance of lists

Descartes presented four precepts to arrive at knowledge. Two are useful here:

'The second, to divide each of the difficulties under examination into as many parts as possible, and as might be necessary for its adequate solution. ...
And the last, in every case to make enumerations so complete, and reviews so general, that I might be assured that nothing was omitted.'

René Descartes, *A Discourse on Method*, 1637 (trans. 2004, John Veitch, Orion Publishing)

Descartes was talking about philosophical analysis, but his advice is sound for more mundane arguments. As you familiarise yourself with your case, note suitable headings for the various elements you might wish to refer to, including: history/chronology; agreed facts; characters involved; issues or disputed facts that need to be addressed; and arguments.

16.1 Planning

This section concerns planning, that is, *what* you are going to say and in what order you are going to say it. *How* you say it is dealt with more fully in Chapters 18 and 20.

The advocacy will take place within a context. You will have goals (direction) that reflect the *issues* you have identified as central to the process. From the outset it is crucial to decide what it is that you want, how this differs from what your opponent wants, and any legal or procedural tests that will be applied to determine the outcome.

The methodology that is to be applied will depend on the nature of the advocacy that you are undertaking. For more formal situations, such as a negotiation, copy the practice of a lawyer and sketch out a skeleton argument. This will help you order your thoughts and it can be handed to your audience, who will find it useful to see how you structure your argument.

16.1.2 Structure

To help your audience follow your argument and make sense of it, a good starting point is to have in mind a classic rhetorical structure.

Illustration 16.2 Rhetorical reference: classical structure

A classical structure is often ordered in the following way:

Exordium

Introduce and establish yourself and your argument with the audience. Create a favourable impression (**ethos** and **primacy**)

Narration and division

Set out the facts and areas of argument in a neutral way. This can include conceding points and identifying **issues** (disputed facts that need to be determined by the process). The narration should have three qualities: brevity, clarity, and plausibility.

Proof and refutation

Having set out the facts and identified the issues, it is time to advance arguments to support your case and to rebut your opponent's. Lawyers refer to these arguments as 'submissions', which can include arguments of analogy, probability and induction (**argument** and **logos**)

Peroration

Bring everything together at the end and invite your audience to find in support of your arguments. Key words or themes developed during your submissions are returned to in the peroration (**clarity** and **stories**)

Whatever structure you opt for do not forget the importance of chronology, which is the most universal and easily understood structure. Ensure that you have a good grasp of the factual chronology and the procedural chronology. Such preparation often reaps rewards as connections are made that may not have been apparent otherwise.

16.1.3 Route planner

The process of advocacy can be likened to a journey. A well-planned route takes into account a number of contingencies, such as road works, weather and traffic conditions.

Your audience will appreciate it if you are able to tell them the route you plan on taking at the outset and the destination you hope to arrive at in due course. So follow the old adage of:

- Tell 'em what you're going to tell 'em
- Tell 'em
- Then tell 'em what you've told 'em.

This approach explains why a well-organised advocate often begins a submission with, 'I will be advancing three key arguments during the course of this morning: A, B, C. If it pleases you, may I begin with A?'

This organisational approach suggests an advocate who is confident (*audacity*) and organised (*organisation*). It also facilitates engagement with the audience as the question 'May I begin?' is not rhetorical and calls for an answer. This is an example of an engineered *pause point*, which is a useful technique to confirm that your audience has followed your last point, prior to proceeding to the next one.

These pause, or transition, points enable an advocate to summarise the gist of their submission to ensure that the audience has taken it on board.

Illustration 16.3 Pause point

Let's imagine that the advocate has just completed their submission with regard to point A: 'So, in summary, my submission here (A) is that the court had no jurisdiction to grant the injunction in the first place. Unless I can help you further, may I move on to my second submission (B)?'

The advocate then pauses and looks to the tribunal for confirmation that they may move on. Unless and until such confirmation is given the advocate should continue to pause. A tribunal often asks a question at this point to clarify their understanding.

Table 16.1 Behavioural evidence of competence: organisation

Organisation qualities	Competent	Not competent
The competent advocate will have prepared well, which will be apparent in the way an argument is introduced and then advanced	• Well structured • Good signposting • Clear agenda (e.g. 'I have three submissions: A, B and C.') • Transition/pause points (e.g. 'Unless I can help you further, may I proceed to my next point?') • Focus on issues/divisions	• 'Master, I have a number of submissions' • 'Also...' • 'In addition...' • 'Finally...' followed by 'finally...' • Poor time management

17 • Clarity

Illustration 17.1 Vorsprung durch Technik (advancement through technology)

You can probably identify these words, used for many years by famous German carmaker Audi. You'll also probably understand their sentiment and ethos, irrespective of your knowledge of German. Interestingly, the advertising executive who came up with this slogan is reported to have said, 'I had no idea that it would become that popular. It says everything and says nothing. That's often the brilliance of a thought, that people put their own meaning in to it.' (Sir John Hegarty, *The Guardian*, 18 September 2012)

As an advocacy objective, clarity has to be a 'no brainer'. Yet how often do we have to listen to a bad advocate struggle to convey their point? Their only hope is that the audience are equipped with extremely good listening skills and a similar level of empathy. However, as we shall see in Chapter 20 Engagement, most people do not have good listening skills and are likely to turn off at the first opportunity. Others may well be irritated by the effort they have to put in to make sense of what is being said.

There are a multitude of reasons why a message may be unclear and it is not possible to provide a solution for each issue. However, the following section sets out three essential strategies for achieving clarity:

1. **Preparation** – fail to prepare, prepare to fail
2. **KIS** – keep it simple

3. **Coherence** – the main thing is to keep the main thing the main thing.

17.1 Preparation: Master the Brief

Rule 1 – and the only rule – is that the advocate must master the brief. Cicero wrote that unless a speaker truly 'grasps and understands what he is talking about, his speech will be worthless.' (*Selected works by Marcus Cicero*, Grant 1960)

Cicero likens the study of a subject to a lawyer taking on a case for a client. They must know *everything*. It has been suggested that good advocacy is 80% preparation. However, preparation is not simply about memorising the facts, it is also about determining how you propose to present your argument and what the essence of your argument is. As mentioned, it is important that you can reduce your argument to a simple proposition. This is not dumbing down but is simply working on how the argument can be made more memorable and coherent. Keep in mind a statement attributed to several famous authors:

> *Sorry about the length of my letter I have not had time to write a shorter one.*

17.2 KIS: Keep it Simple

> *An intellectual ... says a simple thing in a difficult way; an artist ... says a difficult thing in a simple way. (Charles Bukowski, Notes of a Dirty Old Man, 1969)*

Great advocates seem to have the ability to move almost effortlessly from an analytical to a creative mindset. The resulting soundbite, or top line, is what is reported in the press and reverberates around social media.

We may not all have the creative flair of a speech-writer or the ability to turn our prose into poetry, but we can all improve the way in which we reduce our arguments. A good starting point is to try and put what you want to say into the proverbial nutshell.

It is a useful exercise to imagine that your audience asks you to summarise your argument in one minute, literally 60 seconds. Could you do this? The courtroom advocate in Illustration 17.1 could, notwithstanding that the complexities of his case required an opening speech of a number of days.

Illustration 17.2 Nutshell

I can still remember the opening sentences of leading counsel in a case I was defending that related to alleged negligent underwriting, and the sums lost were extremely large. In these opening sentences you will note that the QC borrows a trope from a famous historical character and then sets out a **commonplace** in which he makes reference to how underwriters learn their trade.

'Never in the history of the City of London, has so much of other people's money been lost by the single-handed negligence of one man. The first lesson learnt by every school leaver starting his first job in an insurance firm is that the whole object of the exercise is to transfer the risk of loss from the shoulders of the few to the shoulders of the many. What Mr X did here was precisely the opposite.'

In two short sentences the advocate manages to address both the value of the case in a monetary sense and the level of culpability.

It can be extremely difficult to encapsulate precisely what your argument is. For example, you may have a vision of where you wish to go, but the nature of the argument makes it vulnerable to attack for being too open or nebulous.

17.3 Exaggerating the Case

An inexperienced advocate can complicate their case by over-egging the pudding – or bigging up the case – when the evidence is unlikely to support the submission. Raising the expectations of your audience is dangerous. If the evidence does not subsequently support your argument you are seen as unreliable or untrustworthy (see Appendix A.2 Ethos).

Do not be afraid to qualify any submissions or to address the weaknesses in your case. It is better that you do this than allow your opponent to dwell on the weaknesses at a later stage. Also, be careful how you ascribe motive and/or try to define the character of an individual. Although it may be impactful and noteworthy to suggest that an individual is the 'most evil man on earth', it does raise the bar quite high. Is it necessary to put it that way?

Always put your case at the level that is easiest to establish. For example, you might suggest that a witness to an event is 'simply mistaken in their recollection'. This is a far easier objective than to suggest that the individual is lying through their teeth. Against this, do remember Chapter 14 Audacity. If you must suggest that someone is lying then you need to put it clearly and with conviction. Do not use euphemisms, as in Illustration 17.3.

Illustration 17.3 Audacity

You are concerned with a situation in which you need to challenge the authenticity of something. For example, let's imagine that a contractor who is claiming money from you, has produced a handwritten logbook/record which purports to evidence their attendance at your site on two occasions. Your foreman has no recollection of the contractor or his people coming on site that week. You note that the entry does not follow the usual pattern and is squeezed in at the bottom of the page, which suggests that it could have been entered after the event – and after the dispute arose.

An advocate who weakly suggests that such entries are 'very convenient', or words to that effect, does little to challenge their authenticity and indeed concedes that they could be genuine. It follows that if it is felt that the entries are not what they purport to be then this must be spelt out loud and clear. Perhaps: 'It is our case that these entries are not what they purport to be and that they were made not when it is suggested but at some time after the event when it became clear that there was an issue as to whether these calls had taken place.' The contractor can still rely on the log book but the challenge to its authenticity means they will have to produce other evidence.

Remember, when you wish to nuance your argument you could use paralipsis (see Chapter 15.2.2). For example:

1. 'It is not our case that the defendant was drunk...'
2. 'Many would describe this conduct as bullying...'.

In the first example the implication is that the defendant has been drinking, which leaves the way open to suggest that the defendant's judgement was influenced by alcohol and that their evidence is less reliable than if they had not drunk anything.

In the second example, the advocate is distancing themself from making a direct personal attack on the witness by using a hypotheses. Yet the notion of bullying is clearly being brought into the case.

17.4 Cohere

An argument is more than the description of a phenomenon. Consider Gary Younge's piece on the US Tea Party (*New Statesman*, 8 November 2010), in which he describes them as an 'incoherent group':

> *The 'Tea Party' does not exist. It has no members, leaders, office bearers, headquarters, policies, participatory structures, budget or representatives. The Tea Party is shorthand for a broad, shallow sentiment about low taxes and small government shared by loosely affiliated, somewhat like-minded people. That doesn't mean the right isn't resurgent. It is. But the forces driving its political energy are not those that underpinned its recent electoral success.*

17.5 Rhetorical Reference: Asyndeton

Younge's list in his second sentence is an example of an asyndeton, which is basically a list with the omission of conjunctions. Another famous example comes from Winston Churchill, speaking in the House of Commons in 1938: 'Silent, mournful, broken, Czechoslovakia recedes into darkness.'

An argument must fit together and have its own 'DNA'. To this end, ensure that any inconsistencies in the reasoning are ironed out and that the strongest point is clear throughout.

Management guru Stephen Covey said that the 'main thing is to keep the main thing the main thing', a theme developed further when we consider case theory in Chapters 12 and 19.

Table 17.1 Behavioural evidence of competence: clarity

Clarity qualities	Competent	Not competent
The competent advocate, through a process of painstaking preparation, will produce an argument that is straightforward and clear	• Well prepared • Focused • Succinct • Clear • Coherent • Addresses issues, 'The evidence in this case will clearly establish...' • 'In a nutshell...'	• Obfuscation • Exaggeration • Non-directional • Blagging it • Provokes 'I don't see where this is taking us ...' • Unable to precis; long-winded

18 • Argument

Much of this chapter's content was touched on in Module B, but its objective is to serve as a timely reminder of how such things impact on the presentation of an argument.

Keep in mind that the purpose of most arguments is not to establish the truth but simply to resolve issues and positions. To that end, we should have in mind who carries the burden of proof and what degree of proof is required to succeed. Once that is agreed, the advocate's objective is then to persuade the opponent that their arguments are more persuasive and are more likely to succeed if the matter were to proceed to court.

In more formal forums, such as debates or presentations, as you begin your submission remember the importance of audacity and be confident that you are presenting a strong argument. Engage your audience. Stand proud and never be apologetic, nor make excuses for your arguments (nervous speakers will find advice on how to manage their anxiety in Appendix B).

Always focus yourself and your audience on the issues. These will depend upon the context in which you are arguing. It will help the process if people can at least agree on what they disagree about? In a presentational situation you will have studied the brief and be mindful of what the prospective client requires.

Ensure that the issues are clearly defined and are not muddled. Quantifiable issues (e.g. a requirement to increase turnover by 20%) are generally preferable to qualitative issues (e.g. to increase turnover).

When defining objectives or arguments, perhaps for discussion at a meeting, keep in mind SMART objectives, as explained in Illustration 18.1.

Illustration 18.1 SMART objectives

This business acronym helps define measurable and realistic objectives. It can be helpful when articulating the issues to be addressed:

S = specific (e.g. increase turnover at plant A)

M = measurable (e.g. by 20%)

A = achievable (or agreed)

R = realistic (or relevant)

T = time-bound (or timely, e.g. by year end)

Pointers to practise

When arguing in a commercial context you are more likely to win over your audience if you can set out your objectives in this way.

You can practise this approach whenever you are proposing or arguing about objectives. Try and measure your proposal and get others to do the same. For example, if someone offers to get back to you shortly, press them to agree a concrete date.

This framing of issues is particularly important when planning an argument that may evoke emotions. The requirement in such cases is good judgement coupled with the skill to set out precisely what you want to argue with great care and clarity.

When it is necessary to argue about something value-laden, such as whether conduct was negligent, particularise what you are alleging so that the allegations can form the focus of the argument.

Illustration 18.2 Negligence

If arguing that someone has **negligently** reversed into your car particularise why you are alleging this (e.g. you failed to check before you reversed; you backed out too quickly; you failed to take heed of your warning system).

18.1 Concede Points

The best way of dealing with points that you cannot refute is to concede them. This demonstrates confidence and allows you to focus on the points that you suggest are more important. By conceding points in this way, you will have your audience's ear – and their appreciation.

However, some care is required that the concession does not equate to a formal admission that restricts you from challenging the point in the future. In negotiations concessions should be made 'without prejudice' to your right to resurrect the issue if the matter is not settled.

Illustration 18.3 Rhetorical reference: concession

Concession is the strategy by which the advocate acknowledges or concedes the validity of a point raised by their opponent.

Positional argument can be tiring for an audience so the decision to concede a point can make the advocate look honest, fair and tribunal friendly (a real ethos builder). If you are speaking first this technique allows you to steal some of your opponent's thunder; difficult issues and aspects can then be dealt with on your own terms.

Illustration 18.4 Conceding

> On one occasion an opponent decided to set out no fewer than ten arguments in support of his case. This was far more than he needed, and I thought he should have pruned them down to three, fairly strong, ones. When it was my time to speak, I was confident that I could shoot down each and every one the ten points – a very good feeling! However, I used a better and more engaging strategy:
>
> 'Sir, my friend has raised no fewer than ten points in support of his argument this morning. It may help if, for the purposes of this case, I were to accept that I might have some difficulty in persuading you against five of the points he raises and for that reason, and for the purposes of today's hearing, I am happy to concede these points. However, I do need to address points six, seven and eight and I hope that when I have done so you may decide that you do not need to hear me on points nine and ten.'
>
> This is also an example of using the technique of telling your audience what you are going to tell them...

18.2 Weak Premises Result in Weak Conclusions

As we saw in Chapter 7, an argument is only as strong as its weakest link. An organised opponent will test your reasoning and interrogate your argument by subjecting it to the Kipling questions. If parts of your reasoning process are contested, ensure that you have the evidence to support your point.

If you are generalising remember to qualify your point by, for example, using the correct adverb. Indeed, it can be very persuasive to introduce a generalisation and then work through qualifiers to demonstrate how balanced your argument is. For example, 'I'm not saying that Dave is always late, or that he has never been early, nor am I saying that he is late more often than not, but the fact is that he is late regularly and not a week seems to pass without him turning up late.'

Don't exaggerate too much, and if you are speaking figuratively then say so.

Check that your *cause and effect* arguments are properly framed. Acknowledge that there are several possible causes as to why something has happened, and then focus on why your suggestion as to causation is the most probable.

18.3 Analogy

A good analogy enables us to make sense of the new by reference to the old or familiar, which can be extremely engaging technique. An analogy can change the mood by generating emotion.

Whether an analogy will work depends to a large extent upon the similarity between the example it uses and the example used in the conclusion. For instance, a common analogy in the run-up to the Iraq war was to suggest that allowing Saddam to remain in power was akin to Chamberlain's appeasement of Hitler in the 1930s. However, its weakness lay in contrasting the risk posed to the UK by Saddam as opposed to Hitler, which was a bit of a stretch.

Illustration 18.5 Try this: attacking analogies

When people use an analogy against your position attack the comparison:

'The situations are totally different...'

'We must compare like with like...'

When you wish to use an analogy, make a list of the elements that are similar between the two situations:

'This is exactly what happened last year; we needed goods in a hurry, you didn't answer our emails, you blamed the rail strike, and you exaggerated logistical issues.'

18.4 Remember Clarity

Be concrete and concise. A long-winded advocate irritates an audience.

18.5 Arguing Before Difficult or Challenging People

Those with power and influence can often be challenging to persuade and/or reason with. They generally have high expectations and require concrete evidence to back-up business claims. Difficult or challenging people can be:

- Results and deadline driven
- Intolerant
- Ultimatum giving
- Distant and detached
- Aloof and arrogant
- Short tempered
- Direct and demanding
- Poor listeners.

Research has found that busy, successful people will often relate better to arguments that are results driven and fact and figure oriented, and that are not too reliant upon emotional engagement.

Illustration 18.6 Difficult and/or challenging people

For examples of poor advocacy one need only watch Dragons' Den. Compare and contrast the advocacy used in these two examples of a budding entrepreneur who requires money to manufacture a widget.

Example 1: 'I'm fairly confident that in the fullness of time I may be able to sell these to a wide market and that my turnover will go through the roof. If you give me £100,000 for 30% of the business I will do my best to get you a good return.'

Example 2: 'Upon the basis of my record to date I am very confident that my business will continue to grow from strength to strength. From my last three years' audited accounts, and on the basis of my order book, I can project an annual growth in turnover of about 15% per annum and an increase in my net profit margin from 20% to 25% this year. I calculate my goodwill at about £500,000 based on my present net profit of £75,000'.

18.6 Evidence

As we saw in Chapter 10, a persuasive argument is one built on evidence.

Whether evidence is considered persuasive in a particular case depends upon a number of factors, most of which are a question of common sense. For example, material that is in the public domain and/or material that is considered more or less incontrovertible, will often be acceptable without the need for formal proof; it's not necessary for an advocate to call an expert witness to confirm that London is the capital of England, and your audience might be happy to recognise that snow is more likely to fall in January than in June (consider the important rhetoric concept of *commonplace*).

As we saw earlier an advocate must try and avoid giving evidence themselves and must not be seen as having an interest in the outcome. If they do, they lose their objectivity and *ethos* appeal. Although in everyday arguments our audience is often our opponent and there may be no practical alternative than for the advocate 'to give evidence'. For example, resolving a small dispute when returning an item to a shop.

In formal adversarial situations, such as arguing before a tribunal or a court, the advocate should always bear in mind the risk of inadvertently misleading the tribunal by suggesting something is a fact, when it is neither agreed by the other side nor is capable of being proven. In such situations it is best to qualify what you say at the time you say it: 'It's my client's case that she called to make the reservation at 8.00 pm, although I should say at this point that the issue of the timing of the call – but not the call itself – is in dispute.'

In less formal advocacy situations the advocate may have a little more leeway. Nevertheless, they should try and underpin important premises in their argument with some type of evidence. For instance, 'It was reported in *The Guardian* this week that 4.3 million children live below the poverty line' will carry more weight than just saying, '4.3 million children live below the poverty line'.

If it is possible to get evidence from neutral or impartial people who do not have an interest in the outcome of the argument, so much the better. This is not to say that those with an interest are excluded, as their account may be essential to shed light on the situation (e.g. a mother who witnesses an accident in which her child was injured would of course be required to give evidence).

18.7 Cause and Effect

As we saw in Chapter 11, it is always important to bear in mind that most events have a multitude of different causes, yet people will generally be selective in citing the causes that support their argument. A good advocate will recognise this and will have in mind that it is difficult to rule out all possibilities. It is important to show that the cause identified as responsible for the outcome is the most probable cause. Such a recognition speaks to the advocate's *ethos* appeal, and thus their persuasiveness.

Table 18.1 Behavioural evidence of competence: argument

Argument qualities	Competent	Not competent
The advocate must craft an argument, or case, that is supported by evidence and which is more compelling than the opponent's	<ul><li>Confident but not arrogant</li><li>Concrete premise with supporting evidence</li><li>Clear conclusions</li><li>Prepared to concede so as to focus on key issues</li><li>Coherent</li><li>Has a clear theme</li><li>Has a collaborative approach, 'Unless I can help you?'</li></ul>	<ul><li>'My friend has not produced any case at all'</li><li>Incoherent</li><li>Weak or sloppy analogy, generalisation or cause and effect argument</li><li>Shopping list advocacy (i.e. argues every point and never concedes)</li><li>Arrogant</li></ul>

19 • Stories

19.1 Creative Advocacy

This chapter revisits the references dealt with in Chapter 12 and the way advocates 'contain' the different elements of a case in a coherent form, with storytelling to the fore. Let's begin by reverting to the 'case' of the lady in the image.

Illustration 19.1 Exercise: image of a lady

© Wikimedia Commons/W.E. Hill

You'll recall that the issue is whether the image depicts an elderly or a younger woman. The advocate's task is to persuade the audience that their submissions are more persuasive than their opponent's by offering a plausible, evidence-based explanation. Although the explanation must not stray too far from the underpinning evidence, and must not be too speculative, the advocate is allowed to create a context and offer an explanation that gives vent to a creative side. Illustration 19.2 demonstrates two competing submissions in the case of the image.

Illustration 19.2 Old or young?

An Old Lady Argument

The advocate suggests that the image depicts an elderly woman huddled in her shabby, old, ill-fitting coat, trying to keep out the cold and continues, 'I invite you to focus on her left eye. This tired, wrinkled, baggy eye has, I suggest, seen a lot of life... Not least, at some time – it would appear – a fist that has flattened her nose and knocked out her teeth.'

A Young Lady Argument

This advocate presents the woman in an entirely different way to supports the case that the image depicts a younger woman.

'I invite you to find that this is an image of a voluptuous young beauty. Imagine her at a table in a busy Parisian Café with her lover... She looks coyly away from him, revealing as she does a graceful neck, adorned with nothing other than a blue velvet choker and the hint of her perfect pert nose...'

In this storytelling the advocates apply some light and shade to their descriptions so that their explanation of her age is more persuasive.

This form of insight (i.e. seeing something clearly), often comes after a long period of reflection and as the advocate struggles to find a coherent explanation. It is a similar experience to that of a police officer studying the evidence in a case, who suddenly 'sees' what happened and realises that the explanation has been staring them in the face.

19.2 The Story Process

Tales and stories can have a clearly recognised structure, with a beginning, a middle and an end. We grow up listening to stories and understand that they are good vehicles for explaining things. Political parties are well aware of the power of developing a narrative and telling a compelling story – and they exploit it.

Telling a story is engaging and enables us to tap into emotion and therefore the mood of the audience (see *pathos*)

Stories enable us to see things differently. They provide an explanation based on the evidence. They make sense. Of course, before an advocate can persuade anyone else of their story (argument), they must first be convinced of it themselves!

In the context of a court case, a lawyer prepares to tell a 'story' when delivering the 'closing speech', which is given at the end of the trial after all the evidence has been presented. However, deciding how to 'close' the case will have been occupying the advocate long before that. Indeed, advocates, like police investigators, will begin compiling a 'story board' almost from the outset. It is vital you have a good idea about how you'd describe your case long before you approach negotiation or mediation. It is always a disaster if you enter negotiations with the mindset that you need to settle the case at any cost. Such an attitude will be obvious to your opponent and will result in you faring badly. Instead, enter a negotiation with a detailed grasp of the evidence and a well-developed story in your mind.

The story will emerge during case preparation. Once you have seen it, keep the story metaphor in mind, as it will shape and define the way you handle each part of your case. Particular emphasis should be given to the 'characters' in the case when looking for explanations as to why people have behaved in a particular way.

Finally, keep in mind that a story will continue to evolve and you should be flexible in your approach. An advocate needs to adapt their story to accommodate and explain aspects that the other side will raise in their account.

Table 19.1 Behavioural evidence of competence: storytelling

Storytelling qualities	Competent	Not competent
The advocate must offer an explanation as to why they're going to win and the best form is a 'story'	• Deals with 'characters' and their motives • Is creative and shows some flair and imagination • Engages • Presents a whole story, with a beginning, a middle and an end • The story is unique and adapts to changing circumstances	• Fails to take on board any weakness in their case • Too rational and neglects the emotional side of an argument • Too speculative

20 • Engagement

Our world seems full of argument and disharmony, fuelled by easy access to social media and unfettered by any apparent interest in facts and truth. In such an environment how does an advocate cut through and differentiate their argument, so that it impacts and registers with their audience? This conundrum was considered from a political perspective by J. Nye who pioneered the notion of soft power. Nye's theories are crucial for diplomats and politicians, but all of us can learn how to finesse our arguments by considering how best to frame them – Nye's 'ability to combine hard and soft power into a successful strategy' (*Soft Power: The Means to Success in World Politics*, PublicAffairs 2004).

As we have seen, persuasion depends upon the advocate understanding how the *three pillars of persuasion* impact upon their message or argument (Appendix A.2). The 'hard' element of argument, involves a consideration of *logos* and the need to assert a claim confidently and supported by facts, clearly defined terms and rational reasoning. The 'soft' element of argument calls for a consideration of *pathos* and emotional appeal, through telling a story and resonating with the audience's values and sense of respect and trust.

A well-crafted argument is often the 'iron fist in the velvet glove' (i.e. soft and hard elements), but its impact depends upon how well it is presented and on the *ethos* appeal of the advocate, that is, the extent to which they are trusted and respected.

This chapter focuses on how to improve your engagement with the audience and looks at the qualities that impact upon a speaker's ability. The skill sets and qualities described complement each other and performance in one often depends upon ability in another.

20.1 Always talk to, never at

Advocacy is best thought of as a dialogue or conversation. Even a set-piece speech should be planned and delivered as if you were speaking individually to each audience member.

The golden rule is to talk *to* the audience, never *at* the audience.

Talking *to* is evidenced by the manner in which the advocate respects the audience (i.e. not telling them what to think or do), always pays attention and is ready to re-explain or to address concerns and reply to questions.

Notwithstanding the common sense in this proposition many speakers fail to engage with their audience. If someone says, 'You're lecturing me', 'You're not listening to what I'm saying', or words to that effect, you need to focus on your engagement skills. Illustration 20.1 shows how listening and questioning skills are as important as speaking skills for an advocate.

Illustration 20.1 Socratic method

Socrates understood *soft power* and the need to talk to his students so as to allow them to work things out for themselves. Instead of telling them what they needed to think, he encouraged them in collaborative argumentative dialogue. He focused on asking questions to stimulate thought and engagement. In this way, he was able to control the process while giving his students the impression that they were working things out for themselves.

Asking questions of your audience nearly always
encourages engagement.

Once an advocate has an idea of the audience's concerns,
ambitions and values it is easier to create a rapport and to make
a meaningful connection with them. Illustration 20.2 shows
how the best leaders have a real *feel* for their audience.

Illustration 20.2 Churchill

'We shall not flag or fail. We shall go on to the end. We
shall fight in France, we shall fight on the seas and oceans;
we shall fight with growing confidence and growing strength
in the air. We shall defend our island whatever the cost
may be; we shall fight on the beaches, we shall fight on
the landing grounds, we shall fight in the fields...' Winston
Churchill, June 1940

When Churchill made this famous speech things were going
badly and he was preparing his people for an impending
invasion by the Nazis. At such a time he had to 'rally the
troops' and send a message of resolve and courage that
was coherent, clear and consistent. Although he could not
speak to each Briton individually, his use of the collaborative
'we' and his understanding and appreciation of the British
people enabled him to engineer a real connection, which
both lifted the people and gave them hope, courage and
resolve.

Rhetorical reference: **anaphora**, the repetition of words or
phrases at the beginning of a clause or sentence (e.g. we
shall fight)

20.2 Listening Skills

Listening skills are vital for an advocate. Not only when finding
out what has happened, but also when presenting the case.

Certainly, not listening to your audience pretty soon equates to talking *at* them.

It helps that most audiences are animated. A raised eye, a furrowed brow or a nodding head all speak volumes to the observant advocate. This visual feedback provides an opportunity to assess the effectiveness of the advocacy and to make adjustments as required. The adjustments might be subtle and involve a change of emphasis, or they might be more significant and require you to backtrack to ensure clarity. These adjustments don't often call for any actual dialogue between advocate and audience. Sometimes an audience will ask for clarity and this intervention is often invited by the advocate, who must wait until the audience has had an opportunity to respond. For instance: a lawyer may say to a judge: 'Can I help you further on that point, your honour?'; a person chairing a meeting might say, 'That concludes my points on holiday entitlement. Unless anyone has any questions, I will now move on to the second item on the agenda, which relates to bonuses.'

20.3 Understand Your Audience

The audience's comprehension of the advocate's arguments will correlate with the advocate's understanding of the audience. It is vital to understand where people are 'coming from' – their prejudices, assumptions and values – if you are to evoke empathy and create engagement.

A lawyer advocate will understand how a judge is likely to react to certain submissions. Judges will have prejudices, reflecting the culture and conventions of the court. For example, pressure of work, a conservative outlook and an overarching concern to do justice, will all shape the court's response to a lawyer's submissions.

Wherever you are required to speak, it is essential that you take steps to understand the context and culture that your audience subscribe to. This includes a consideration of any prejudices or beliefs particular to that audience. This advice should be fairly obvious but experience dictates that people often fail to do the research. Illustration 20.3 shows how such ignorance can damage engagement.

Illustration 20.3 Advocacy coach: pitch preparation

I was helping a legal team prepare a pitch for work from a global utility company. At one stage I began asking questions of the prospective pitchers that related to quite esoteric but nevertheless important aspects of the target's business. Their level of ignorance surprised me. How were they going to be able to engage with and impress an organisation if they had not taken steps to ascertain vital facts and figures on the business? Their focus had been on what the team had to offer, while the details of the prospective client's business had been glossed over.

20.4 Persuasion Requires Seduction

An advocate should always have in mind the *autonomy* of the audience and remember that the objective is to *persuade* them, not to c*ontrol* or *command* them. People do not respond well to being told how they should think or what they should decide. They need to be 'sold' the idea or argument. It helps to think of persuasive advocacy as that which *seduces* or *pulls* the audience toward the conclusion, not that which *pushes* or *instructs* them. Push too hard and the audience will dig their heels in and harden their opposition to the argument. The notion of soft power referred to above is an example of a collaborative and non-controlling approach.

Illustration 20.4 contains examples of pulling and pushing.

Illustration 20.4 Push and pull

Pushing Bad

'If you want to do justice you have no option but to find for my client.'

'Only a fool would disagree with my argument'.

In these examples the advocate is forgetting that they have to persuade their audience. The suggestion that someone has 'no option' is aggressive and crass (unless a gun is being held to a head!). Telling someone that they are foolish for not agreeing with you demonstrates a complete ignorance of what argument is.

Pulling Good

'On the basis of these three points I would invite you to conclude...'

'That is the basis of my case. I would be pleased to answer any questions you may have...'

We all prefer an invitation to a command and a reasoned argument to an unsubstantiated claim. We also like to be involved in the process and to have our queries addressed.

Illustration 20.5 Get to the back of the queue

During the UK EU referendum campaign in spring 2016, Barack Obama was on a trip to London and sought to bolster the remain campaign by suggesting that leaving could mean that the UK would have to 'get to the back of the queue' to negotiate a post-exit trade deal with the USA. Following this intervention, the polls picked up a swing to the 'out' camp, which was the opposite of what had been intended. Many political observers felt that Obama's 'push' intervention was construed as a threat to the British people, who reacted by hardening their resolve to leave the EU. Perhaps he could have been more persuasive had he been less abrupt and just pointed out that any post-exit trade deal would be likely to take some time to negotiate.

20.5 Persuasion Depends Upon Trust

An audience will not be persuaded by an advocate that they do not trust.

As Illustration 20.5 showed, trust can be lost if an advocate appears overtly partisan. Another danger lies in misleading your audience. This could be a deliberate lie, but it is possible to mislead inadvertently, for example by negligently or carelessly allowing an audience to believe something is the case when it is not. An advocate who believes that an audience has the wrong end of the stick should quickly ensure that they are corrected. Any advocate who is responsible for misleading their audience should apologise.

20.6 Expressing an Opinion

A trustworthy advocate is clear, confident and unequivocal. They are also careful not to express an opinion as if it were a fact. Apart from being wrong, such an assertion can easily create a negative response, and thus become a distraction. For example, an advocate who claims that it is always wrong to lie is almost guaranteed to be met by, 'Then it's wrong to tell children that Father Christmas is real.' That's a fair point, but it may disengage or derail the speaker or the audience from the point that was being made (i.e. that it is wrong to lie). These sorts of distractions can be avoided by careful qualification of the proposition, for instance, 'I would suggest that there are very few situations where it is right to lie.' Such a framing should keep the Father Christmas objector quiet.

An advocate will take care that arguments are not too dogmatic, to avoid the risk of being considered prescriptive or inflexible. In such cases people disengage very quickly and spend time considering ways in which they can attack or qualify the advocate's position. Avoid this by looking carefully at how you frame your argument. For example, although it is possible to argue unequivocally that young children should not be given loaded guns to play with, that same certainty cannot be relied upon when arguing that religious education should be compulsory for schoolchildren.

20.7 Avoiding Positional Arguments

An advocate should focus on their *ethos* appeal, in particular the need to build a reputation as being fair and reasonable. One way of doing this, and of demonstrating an understanding of the complexity of argument, is to concede.

The adversarial nature of arguments means that people can become positional, stop listening and lose the ability to reason. Matters can quickly become personal and the issues that need to be addressed can be forgotten as the argument takes on a life of its own. A good example of this is Prime Minister's Question Time in the House of Commons when both sides go hammer and tongs at each other and believe that any concession will be seen as a sign of weakness. However, to most third-party observers, an advocate who is prepared to concede a point comes across as reasoned and fair-minded. In Chapter 18.1 we saw that conceding ground is an extremely engaging and persuasive thing to do.

What can be conceded depends upon context, but a good advocate will have in mind that 'we have more in common than that which divides us', and will sweep aside non-contentious points so the argument focuses on the important issues.

Illustration 20.6 Sensible concessions

The concession has to make sense. It would be daft to concede the very point that was to be argued (e.g. 'I am going to argue that we should remain in the EU, but I concede that it would be best for us to leave.'). However, an advocate wanting to base an argument on the perceived economic benefits of remaining in the EU, might be able to demonstrate a degree of objectivity and boost ethos appeal by saying, 'I accept that there are many things wrong with the EU. People are concerned by immigration, which is high, they are worried about the level of bureaucracy, which is excessive, and they do wonder about some European Court judgments. Yet it is my argument that the economic benefits of remaining in far exceed some of the problems that I accept we need to address.'

In effect, the advocate is saying that although there may be many issues, the key issue – in their view – is the economy. This illustration shows how concession may be used in a debate when each advocate is trying to demonstrate their fairness or good judgement to the audience.

20.8 Building and Maintaining Rapport

Engagement is about creating some degree of rapport with an audience. We have seen that the best way to achieve this is for the advocate to *talk to* their audience and *listen carefully* to what they say.

People's attention spans are short. Although some (such as judges) are better than others, all audiences are human and need to be encouraged to listen. The issue, therefore, is how to gain and keep attention. *Primacy* suggests that an audience's attention is likely to be higher as an advocate begins to speak and dips soon after. Build your rapport with the audience during the early honeymoon period.

Delivering a presentation can be nerve-wracking and there is always a risk of an advocate losing their way. When this happens an audience is generally sympathetic, provided the advocate comes clean and does not try and dismiss the difficulty, or fudge a response. In such a case, ask your audience 'for a minute' and take stock before proceeding. You can also take the opportunity to deploy the rhetorical technique of *aporia* to address the situation.

Illustration 20.7 Rhetorical Reference: aporia, I'm not sure

Aporia describes a situation when the advocate admits that they do not know the answer to a question. Admitting ignorance can, if handled with care, create a rapport with your audience as they will often try and resolve the issue with you.

'To be quite frank, I'm not sure what the position would be in that case.'

This is a much better technique than simply trying to blag it, as an audience in such a case will quickly lose confidence in you.

It can be difficult to maintain a rapport if you are faced with a hostile audience. Try not to fall back on 'don't shoot the messenger'. This approach can isolate an audience and make your task harder. Try and resist the temptation to argue with the audience and instead seek out common ground. This is an important negotiating technique. Illustration 20.8 shows how an advocate can reframe an argument by picking up and focusing on agreed common ground. This technique is akin to a skilful cross-examination in which the advocate asks leading questions to direct the witness to where they want them to be.

Illustration 20.8 Rhetorical reference: reframing around common values

A: 'The unemployed are bone idle and should get off their backsides and go out and find work!'

B: 'I assume that you believe that working is the right thing to do?'

A: 'Too bloody right!'

B: 'And that doing a job of work defines a person and gives them purpose?'

A: 'Has done with me!'

B: 'To be industrious, hardworking and a breadwinner makes one feel good doesn't it?'

A: 'Sure does.'

B: 'I guess that without that purpose in your life you might feel bereft and at a loss.'

A: 'But I wouldn't be without work, I'm a striver.'

B: 'I'm sure you are, but what if you were ill and housebound? How do you think you'd you feel then?'

A: 'Depressed.'

B: 'Do you know that there is a high suicide rate among young unemployed men? Many must feel very low.'

20.9 How to Disengage Your Audience

The best way to disengage an audience is not to research their culture and values, and not to bother adapting your presentational style and decorum to reflect what they will expect. Such a careless approach makes it is likely that the advocate will have a problem dealing with the audience's prejudices.

Many young advocates and advocacy workers use terms and expressions that can alienate them from their audience. While these behaviours may not be wrong, in certain situations they can *distract*.

Many prejudices are ingrained and are hard to address. Others can be dealt with more easily. Illustration 20.9 highlights just a few examples of behaviour that can irk and disengage an audience.

Illustration 20.9 Disengaging behaviour

Avoid vocabulary that will disengage or irritate your audience.

Obviously: is used by some to mean 'of course' (which is itself pretty annoying). It is often used as a filler to hold the audience's attention – 'I had a car crash last night and obviously I can't get to work today and, obviously, I have a claim.'

Like: this started in North America as a vocalised pause equivalent to 'um' or 'er' – 'It is, like, really aggravating to, like, anyone over 50 when, like, you keep saying like all the time.'

Americanisms: language changes and I'm not suggesting that you should never use American expressions. In a large international firm they'd be acceptable, but that might not be the case in a smaller, regional firm. For instance, using restroom or the American pronunciation for leisure or schedule.

Strive to use words and phrases that do not sound like 'management speak', unless your audience expects and understands the jargon. Fashions do change, and words and expressions – usually American – become part of the language. It is not a bad idea to check the internet from time to time to see which words or phrases are annoying Plain English evangelists. Table 20.1 shows some words that the Local Government Association discouraged their members from using in March 2010, with suggested alternatives.

Table 20.1 Alternative words

Dialogue	Talk/discuss
Exemplar	Example
Going forward	In the future
Interface	Talking to each other
Joined up	Working together
Outcomes	Results
Procure	Buy
Promulgate	Spread

Of course, linguistic fashions change and this list is simply to show how important it is to make an effort to empathise and 'tune in'.

20.10 Summary

This chapter looked at the crucial importance of striving to 'talk to and not at', which is best achieved by adopting a conversational style.

Active listening is an engaging technique that builds a rapport with, and commands the respect of, those you are communicating with. It also ensures that you truly understand your audience, which must always precede seeking to influence and persuade them.

To maintain attention we must try and avoid distracting arguments and disagreements over peripheral points. One technique to achieve this is to concede as much as you can and to frame matters so that you can control the agenda.

Table 20.2 Behavioural evidence of competence: engagement

Engagement qualities	Competent	Not competent
Advocate talks to the audience and in doing so creates rapport Advocate understands and empathises with the audience and assists them in their deliberations	• Talks to audience • Empathises • Collaborative dialogue (e.g. use of pronoun 'we') • Honest (e.g. **aporia**) • Conversational in nature • Open body language • Listens intently and uses active listening skills and questions • 'Invites' audience to find • 'Pulls' • Understands to be understood • Recognises prejudices • Concedes and frames issues that are important	• Talks at audience • Instructional monologue • Interrupts audience • Dogmatic • Disengaged body language • Injunctive • 'Pushes' • Knows little about audience's culture and probably cares less • Argues positionally • Distracts by invoking prejudice (e.g. semantics)

Appendices

Appendix A   •
Rhetorical Notes

Contents

A.1 Introduction: Why Rhetoric?

> *'Better to remain silent and be thought a fool than to speak out and remove all doubt.' Abraham Lincoln*

A.1.1 The X factor

What qualities do good advocates or speakers have? Is it possible to identify precisely what it is they do and how they do it? What makes them stand out?

It is not easy to identify such qualities. Good speakers share many attributes with the rest of us, such as a regular-sized brain, a vocabulary of about 20,000 words and a capacity to speak about 180 words per minute. They don't show distinctive physical attributes and there is little, physiologically, to differentiate the 'good and the great' from the rest of us.

So, why such a gulf in performance? What is their X factor and can such qualities and attributes be learnt?

When I've asked for examples of a good speaker's qualities, people have suggested the following:

- Top speakers are charismatic and eloquent and have an ability to engage, influence and persuade
- They can effortlessly hold the attention of an audience and can be trusted to make sense and say what is required at the time, and no more
- Leadership
- Great speakers have confidence and flair
- They have an ability to make that which is complex appear straightforward.

These answers are all broadly descriptive of the phenomena that mark out a competent speaker. Yet these descriptions alone do little to shed light on what has to be *learnt* by anyone keen to emulate these individuals.

Perhaps Aristotle wrestled with this conundrum in the fourth century, before he formulated his seminal *Treatise on Rhetoric*. Aristotle's treatise is almost certainly the most important single work on persuasion ever written, and is widely regarded as influencing the development of rhetorical theory from antiquity through to contemporary times. It is hard to think of a better place to begin building your speaking skills.

A.1.2 Rhetoric's role in building the X factor

An understanding of some core rhetorical principles can have a positive impact on a speaker's competence and confidence. Such insights do not require an in-depth knowledge of Hegelian dialectic, nor a recognition of the difference between *hypophora* and *erotesis*, but simply an appreciation of some core rhetorical principles. The rhetorical content in this book is practical, sensible and easy to digest. Furthermore, having withstood the scrutiny of more than 2,000 years, it is hard to think of a better foundation upon which to build your expertise.

A.1.3 What is rhetoric?

Rhetoric is simply the art of persuasion. It focuses on planning what you want to say, in what order and how you are going to say it.

As what we say reflects what we are thinking, it helps to regard rhetoric as an analytical reasoning skill as much as a presentational skill.

Many of Aristotle's terms, tropes, tools and techniques have become part of everyday speech – alliteration, analogy, antithesis, metaphor, hype and eulogy, to name but a few.

Appendix A will give you rhetorical perspectives that can quickly benefit and make a positive impact upon your speaking performance.

A.2 Three Pillars of Persuasion: Appeals to Gut, Heart and Head

A.2.1 Introduction

People often refer to different parts of their anatomy when describing how they are influenced; they may say that their head tells them one thing and their heart another, but that their gut tells them something else.

It may have been these anatomical perspectives that led Aristotle to describe three different types of persuasive appeal (often referred to as the three pillars of persuasion) known as ethos, pathos and logos. He suggests we should bear each one in mind whenever we are planning to inform, influence or persuade. They have as much relevance today as they did when formulated 2,000 years ago.

This section (A.2.2–4) provides a brief overview of each pillar, while sections A.3–A.5 explain them in more detail.

A.2.2 Ethos: building your credibility; gut instinct

- 'People speak highly of her. She certainly seems to know what she's talking about'
- 'I like her attitude she talks a lot of common sense and wants to help'
- 'She certainly understands where we are coming from. I trust her judgement'

Ethos tells us how to establish and build credibility. Aristotle identified several issues that help build credibility and suggested that an ethos appeal targets the audience's gut instincts.

A.2.3 Pathos: emotional appeal; pulling on heart strings

- 'Her talk certainly fired up the Board'
- 'After she finished speaking there was not a dry eye in the house'
- 'They seem to be running a fear campaign'

Pathos relates to how far the speaker can alter the mood of an audience. A charitable campaign will often play on a pathos appeal in their images, music and words, which will be calculated to impact on the audience's emotions.

A.2.4 Logos: rational; appeals to reasoning

- 'What she's saying makes sense'
- 'It's clear what she's getting at'
- 'The evidence does seem to stack up in her favour'

Logos looks to the intellectual appeal of an argument – the reasoning processes that we looked at in Module B. Its name derives from logic but, unlike logic, it is not concerned with uncovering the 'truth,' it simply addresses probabilities.

Logos relates to the rationality of an argument. We saw in earlier chapters how important it is that an argument stacks up and is supported by relevant evidence, facts and premises.

A.2.5 Summary

Aristotle said that each of the three pillars – ethos, pathos and logos – were equally important parts of the same 'building' and should all be kept in mind. People may listen to you because of your reputation (ethos), be engaged by your use of emotions and mood changing (pathos), and then justify their support for you on logical grounds (logos).

In my training and coaching experience, I have found that people have a tendency to focus on one pillar and are not easily persuaded to consider the others. Illustration A.2.1 relates to a young lawyer who found it hard to understand why the speaker's credibility or the audience's emotion should have any bearing upon the planning and delivery of a legal argument. In his defence, he had been schooled in the need to focus on facts and rationality when arguing, that is, on the logos pillar.

Illustration A.1 Advocacy coach: rhetoric and logical fallacy

A bright young lawyer I was working with challenged me on why a speaker should focus on either his own 'credibility' or the 'emotion' of the audience. He argued (well) that such an approach could distract from the 'proper intellectual thrust' of an argument. An argument, he suggested, should be rationally focused and fact based. It followed that rhetoric devices such as ethos and pathos seemed, at best, logical fallacies (flaws in reasoning by use of tricks and mirrors) or, at worse, unethical. In his view, rhetoric was not something that lawyers should contemplate.

Although I readily agreed that fallacious argument was always to be avoided, I did not accept that Aristotle's notions were either irrational or unethical. I explained that Aristotle considered himself a pragmatist who concerned himself with **persuasion**, which generally turns on issues of **probability** and not the **truth**. I did concede that the emphasis in building a legal argument should be upon facts and rationality (logos), but I pointed out that advancing and 'winning' that argument (perhaps at a negotiation) will often depend equally upon emotion (pathos) and reputation (ethos). The last two also help to explain the conduct and behaviour of third parties involved in the dispute and can form an important part of the advocate's case theory.

Sections A.3–A.5 look more carefully at ethos, pathos, and logos, and demonstrate how each has a real bearing on our ability to connect with and to 'sell' an argument or point of view to an audience.

A.3 Ethos: Credibility

A.3.1 Ethos in a nutshell

Aristotle considered ethos the most important of the three persuasive appeals. Ethos relates to the apparent credibility, character and authority of a speaker. It is often broken down into three elements:

- **Virtue** – do the speaker's values 'fit' or 'reflect' the audience's?
- **Practical wisdom** – does the speaker know what he is talking about?
- **Disinterested goodwill** – can the speaker be trusted?

As you work through this section bear in mind that ethos considerations apply not only to your credibility as an advocate or influencer, but also to the credibility of those you rely upon in furtherance and/or support of your argument (e.g. witnesses).

Also reflect upon how these considerations bear upon the reputational impact of your organisation. Organisations could certainly build a more credible reputation by improving their corporate ethos appeal.

Aristotle's basic proposition was that a speaker's good reputation is itself persuasive. We shall now consider the three elements which he considered most important.

A.3.2 Virtue or values

Good advocates make it their business to ascertain as much as possible about the cultural values and mores of their audience. If the advocate can demonstrate that they share some of these defining values, they are far more likely to be accepted as 'one of us', and to be considered reliable. It makes sense to try and modify your approach to show that you empathise with your audience and share some of their beliefs and customs. This need not be a highbrow approach. For example, I would often create some degree of rapport with taxi drivers in Athens by finding the first opportunity to drop into conversation a popular Greek swear word (see Illustration A.3). Although not typically a virtuous thing to do in the grand scheme of things, my choice of profanity suggested I was not 'wet behind the ears' and perhaps – among other things – knew the most direct route to the hotel!

On the other hand, we must be cautious not to come across as sycophantic or disingenuous, as our 'virtue' will go out of the window the instant we appear insincere or contrived. For example, a leading politician's attempt to portray himself as a football fan came unstuck when he seemed confused over whether he was a West Ham or an Aston Villa supporter (they wear similar colours). A football supporter would consider such a mix-up as akin to forgetting what religion you follow.

Illustration A.2 Advocacy watch: values

A great example of someone coming unstuck for not having properly understood the values of his audience is Tony Blair during his speech to the Woman's Institute in 2000. Notwithstanding having been warned that the WI was a non-political organisation that would not tolerate political point scoring, Blair strayed into political content (e.g. NHS reform and interest rate cuts) and was roundly heckled and slow handclapped. When he adapted his approach and made reference to such matters as the role and responsibilities of fatherhood and help for mothers with young children, he was more politely received. The moral is: do your homework into the culture of those you'll be addressing or risk getting your fingers burned.

Illustration A.3 Try this: virtue or values; virtue words

A rhetorical technique that demonstrates shared values is known as a **virtue word**. Virtue words are often used in politics – and advertising – and can signify that you 'speak the speak' and share a value with your audience (e.g. human rights, war on terror or bureaucracy). Such terms are generally context specific and relate to a particular culture or group (see also **commonplaces**).

If you wish to impress a particular organisation, then checking out their website, social media and literature to identify common virtue words they use is time well spent. These can then be included in your dialogue with them. Of course, subtlety is required as an audience will know if you are being sycophantic or fawning – as always, judgement is called for.

The trick is to pick up the expressions and words that organisations rely on in describing their business, organisation or culture. For example:

• In a pitch to a global company that describes its global structure as polycentric: 'I appreciate that as a polycentric organisation it is important that your suppliers understand ...'

• In a report to a client whose HR Director is a keen advocate of organisational learning, 'We believe organisational learning is essential for any innovative business...'

A.3.3 Practical wisdom: phronesis

An audience will perceive a speaker with *practical wisdom* as intelligent and reliable, as imbued with common sense and discernment. Such people are often leaders in their field and are likely to be seen by their audience as good or virtuous. Donald Trump was thought by many to have a real 'understanding of things', as evidenced by his earlier success in business (others were not so confident in his abilities).

• How can I demonstrate that I have practical wisdom?

- What are the characteristics of people with such a quality?

Banging on about your PhD may persuade people that you are clever, but that alone is unlikely to persuade them of your *practical wisdom.*

People with practical wisdom are able to demonstrate real and relevant *experience* which shapes their decision-making process. It is for that reason that business leaders are often considered to have this quality, provided they are commenting on matters that flow from their experience. It follows that although I may listen carefully to what Richard Branson has to say about business start-ups, I may not be so persuaded by his views on baking – when I'd put greater store on that fount of wisdom, Mary Berry!

If you wish to display your practical wisdom you should frame your answer, or view point, by reference to your experience. Clearly, the greater the relevant experience, the greater your potential *practical wisdom.* Illustration A.3 tells an apocryphal story concerning George Carman, QC – probably one of the finest courtroom advocates of the twentieth century.

Illustration A.4 Advocacy watch: experience – George Carman, QC

The setting for this story is a chance meeting between Carman and Tiny Rowland, an industrialist and former client of Carmen's. Rowland was embroiled in a well-publicised and expensive trial in the High Court, in which Carman was not involved. As they exchanged pleasantries in the street outside the courts one lunchtime, Rowland is alleged to have asked Carman for his opinion on who was likely to win the litigation he was involved in. History has it that Carman replied to the effect, 'Well I'm not following it that closely but in my experience of these types of cases, I fear that you are going to lose on this occasion.'

The next day Rowland received a £500 fee note from Carman's Chambers for 'Advice given in The Strand relating to merits of case'. When Rowland rang to protest and report that the conversation had taken no longer than a couple of minutes, the Clerk responded by saying that when Mr Carman was asked to opine, and did so, his opinion was never worth less than £500.

Quite the demonstration of the (real) value of being seen to have practical wisdom!

It may not be possible to demonstrate your practical judgement with a yes or no answer as the complexities of life's problems generally require a more nuanced and measured response. A more realistic answer to a complex problem is often, 'It depends ...'. Such an answer implicitly rejects the possibility of there being one straightforward answer to a question, which most sensible people already know. A confident advocate is not afraid of couching views in this way as it suggests relevant experience is being brought to bear upon the problem.

So, instead of trying to be too positional, steer a *middle course* and be prepared to concede certain aspects, safe in the knowledge that this is more likely to enhance your position than to weaken it. Much of this depends upon your ability to reason well (see Module B).

Illustration A.5 Try this: practical wisdom; the middle ground

In an adversarial situation, consider adopting a balanced moderate position. Most people recognise that a just outcome generally lies somewhere between two extreme positions. Watch the way political grandees appear confident to concede points and acknowledge (some) weakness in their own position. Be prepared to demonstrate your confidence and judgement and your willingness to try and get to the bottom of an issue. As a consequence, you are more likely to be seen as fair and reasonable.

Examples:

1. 'I readily accept that we should have done better here and that the contract documents arrived a day later than they should have done but we are where we are'

2. 'Your guess is probably as good as mine'

3. 'It is difficult to predict with certainty precisely what the position will be after we pull the contract but my view is...'

A.3.4. Disinterested goodwill: selflessness

Lawyers are seen as conflicted and unable to represent someone in court if they have a financial or other interest in the outcome of the hearing. The regulatory thinking behind this rule is that an advocate should be free of any temptation to behave in a way that might enrich him or her, at the cost of the client.

Similar considerations apply to politicians, who have to disclose details of their financial affairs so that their neutrality and objectivity can be gauged and vetted.

These examples demonstrate what we all know, that our arguments will be more persuasive if our audience trusts us and sees that our judgements are not clouded by vested interests.

Aristotle uses the expression *disinterested goodwill* to describe how advocates can enhance their ethos by ensuring that their audience appreciate that they have no personal interest in the outcome of the argument.

It follows that you should, at all times, strive to adopt an independent and professional approach, and in so doing demonstrate your independence of thought and objectivity.

• How can I be objective in an argument?

- Isn't the whole process adversarial?

Of course, we all have our biases when arguing, but the secret is to manage any prejudice by steering away from adversarial and one-sided positions. Striving to occupy the middle ground suggests reasonableness, wisdom and judgement. For example, a good salesperson in a clothes shop may persuade you not to buy an ill-fitting suit, which builds up your trust in their objectivity. As a consequence you are more likely to be loyal to the shop over the longer term. Another example of disinterestedness is a well-known life insurance company which advertised that their sales people were not paid a commission on business they placed. The idea was to encourage prospective clients to trust in the judgement and objectivity of the sales people; they were not selling you a product simply to receive a commission but they wanted what was best for you.

Illustration A.6 Try this: selflessness

Freely admit and concede to any element of self-interest or bias in an argument. This not only prevents the other side from using it as a stick to beat you with, but it also shows how fair and open-minded you are.

Behave as if you are really trying to take into consideration the other side's argument: 'Help me understand your point.'

Do not simply reflect on building your own ethos appeal but look at how you can attack and undermine your opponent's: 'What is your commission on this deal?' 'Would you like to tell us who your wife works for?'

Subtlety is required with all these techniques to avoid coming across as insincere: 'Look, I'm cutting off my nose to give you this deal and I will probably be fired on Monday but ...'

Appear reluctant to address something that, in reality, is an issue you wish to focus on, 'I hoped that we would not need to talk about your punctuality but as you have brought it up, I feel I must make a few points.'

A.3.5 Ethos in practice

As part of their preparation smart advocates carefully evaluate the potential prejudices of an audience and the impact they'll have on their own credibility. They can then use their judgement to conclude whether or not they are the right person to win over that audience on that particular occasion.

Illustration A.7 Advocacy watch: ethos; establishing credibility

Owen Jones (a left-wing journalist) once told me of his surprise (and relief) at the reaction of a middle-class, market town audience to his arguments for being hard on tax avoiders and utility companies. Although in the main the audience had little enthusiasm for Owen's political position, they nevertheless appreciated the clarity and focus of some of his arguments and the confident way in which they were advanced.

Preparation is crucial. I still remember cleaning my shoes and ironing my shirt with extra care the night before I was due to appear before a judge I'd been told had expressed the view that, 'a scruffy advocate seldom produces a tidy argument'. But ethos appeal and credibility do not depend entirely on presentational performance. A nervous advocate can impress with their credibility as much as a confident performer. Indeed, Cicero believed that those with no fear of public speaking should feign at least a little anxiety so as to maintain engagement with their audience. He claimed that Crassus (another great Roman orator) feigned diffidence so he did not appear aloof or superior to his audience.

Illustration A.8 Rhetorical reference: dubitatio

'A speaker might choose to feign helplessness by pretending to be uncertain how to begin or proceed with his speech. This makes him appear not so much as a skilled master of rhetoric, but as an honest man.' Quintilian

It may be that you have no need to feign helplessness or anxiety, but it is reassuring to bear in mind that an audience will generally be sympathetic to an anxious speaker, provided that it is apparent they have prepared well.

A.3.6 How to build ethos appeal

Reputations take a long time to build and a short time to lose. Bear in mind the following to ensure that you begin to build yours effectively and immediately.

A.3.6.1 Things to work on continuously

- Create good karma or, if you prefer, be virtuous. Understand that your behaviour may come back to haunt you. Always remember that audiences can be very judgemental and will not quickly forget an advocate's attempt to mislead them, even if this appears to have happened innocently. Such lapses will reflect badly, not only on the advocate but also on the advocate's organisation.
- Become an expert and strive to differentiate yourself from others. Promote yourself on LinkedIn. Join trade and professional organisations. Write blogs on topics that you may need to speak on.

- Promote yourself or, better still, get somebody else to do it. Being the world's authority on fine wines will not of itself grow your ethos appeal unless and until people know of this expertise. Remember that ethos concerns people's perceptions of you, so you need to market yourself. Create a brand that emphasises the qualities you want to promote and bear in mind that being unduly modest is not always a good strategy (note Donald Trump and José Mourinho).
- Make it your responsibility to fully understand your audience and its culture. If you are summoned to appear before the House of Commons Public Accounts Committee, wear a tie or risk looking arrogant. If, on the other hand, you are visiting the troops at the front you can probably leave the tie at home. Try to fit in (see A.3.7 Decorum).

A.3.6.2 Things to bear in mind **before** *making a speech or presentation*

- Respect your audience by turning up on time and in the right attire.
- Understand to be understood. Your research should focus on the audience's culture and/or recent events that relate to their business or organisation. Check out their website and read their latest press releases. If speaking at a conference or meeting, listen to what is said before you speak and pick up references and themes that can be developed or referred to when it is your turn.
- Make reference to your reputation in any marketing materials you may be distributing and in the introduction to your speech. If someone is to introduce you make sure they have a biography that includes those aspects you

want mentioned. It is always better to have a third party 'blow your trumpet'!

*A.3.6.3 Things to bear in mind **during** the speech or presentation*

- Try and be consistent. Avoid contradicting yourself.
- Try and use language that is appropriate to the forum you are addressing. For example, the proper use of acronyms can demonstrate that you are in tune with the jargon and culture of your audience. However, incorrect usage risks undermining your reputation.

Illustration A.9 Advocacy coach: prep for talking the talk

A newly qualified lawyer wanted to shine at an interview for an M&A role at a leading City firm. He asked for some advice on how he might prepare. I told him that it is always dangerous to exaggerate your experience, but that it is sensible to show you at least understand some of the jargon. I recommended that before the interview he should study global law firm Latham & Watkins' helpful **Book of Jargon® – Global Mergers & Acquisitions**. It explains 'blue book', 'squeeze out', 'bump', 'poison pill', 'PIPE' and many other esoteric terms.

The use of such jargon is an example of **metonymy**. Although it may be tempting to show off by using esoteric terms it is important that you understand them. The same thinking applies to avoiding words your audience is unlikely to understand.

A.3.7 Decorum

It's not sensible to discuss ethos without referencing the notion of *decorum*, which relates to the ability to fit in with your audience – your 'street cred' and style. This has a lot to do with culture and it helps explain why lawyers still wear wigs and gowns in a court of law and why MPs bray at each other across the despatch box in the House of Commons.

If you are going to address an unfamiliar group (e.g. at a new client pitch), it is essential to learn as much as you can about your target audience's style and culture. This will help you plan arguments and propositions that are more likely to fit, or connect.

The idea of decorum also goes some way to explaining the rhetorical phenomena of political correctness or, more recently, being woke. Many of us will be concerned to ensure that we continually adapt our language and the way in which we frame an argument, to reflect the environment in which we are speaking. Those who complain about political correctness may secretly be lamenting (or be assumed to be lamenting) inevitable changes in the social environment.

When considering decorum, one size does not fit all. For example: Jeremy Clarkson is not all at concerned about offending some people, as reactionary silliness is part of his ethos appeal as an entertainer; Dominic Cummings appears to want to create a 'too cool for school' look with his apparent contempt for traditional office apparel. Indeed, Cicero recognised diversity of style and personality when he advised that you should not try and assume a character that strays too far from your own. If you do, there is a real danger that your audience will pick up on your falsity – their gut tells them you're faking it. Good examples are politicians trying to speak 'estuary' English or someone talking up (or down) their class or background.

It is important to show respect to your audience and their cultural values. This no doubt explains why Mark Zuckerberg abandoned his usual T-shirt and jeans for a formal business suit and tie when summoned to give evidence before a Committee of US senators in April 2018. To do otherwise would have risked appearing disrespectful of his audience.

Illustration A.10 Advocacy coach: working on your decorum

Young advocates sometimes ask my advice on how they should address such 'issues' as regional dialect or concerns they have about their background/class. History is full of examples of how people have addressed their perceived decorum shortcomings: Margaret Thatcher felt that her pitch was too shrill; Harold Wilson believed that a pipe would be more working class than his favoured cigars; Labour MP Michael Meacher sued a newspaper for suggesting that he was 'middle class'.

My advice is to embrace who you are, where you come from and what you have done. There is nothing as off-putting as people faking it. Figures such as Boris Johnson or Jacob Rees-Mogg are far better off honestly affirming (and embracing) their upper-class background than trying to conceal it – and the same applies to 'working-class heroes' such as Alan Sugar.

However, you can and should try to **fit in** if doing so does not compromise your values or beliefs. There is no sense in not dressing in a way that your audience expects, and any good advocate will always be respectful of their audience.

A.4 Pathos: Addressing Emotion

A.4.1 Introduction

Pathos is the quality of a persuasive presentation that appeals to the emotions. For example, the advocate may wish to exploit anger or fear, at which times the audience's decision-making process may be less rational. In other situations, the advocate may wish to calm the audience's mood to focus on rational arguments. In either case it is important to recognise how emotion plays a part in the communication process and how the speaker can use these insights to their own ends.

Illustration A.11 Advocacy watch: emotion

1. In the summer of 2015, the tragic image of a child's body washed up on a shore in Turkey did more to engage the public with the horrors of the refugee crisis than any number of broadsheet leaders. As a direct consequence of the image, and sensing the mood of the nation, the Government softened its stance and agreed to a greater number of refugees being allowed into the UK.

2. Allegations of 'project fear' were levelled at both the Remain and Leave camps during the Brexit Referendum. Questions were raised as to whether these tactics were effective during the campaign.

Pathos is the strategic use of emotion to engage with and influence your audience. The emotion can be your own or your audience's. As a strategy, pathos is much more than a mawkish or sentimental appeal for sympathy. It is not restricted to the spoken word and it can extend to the use of imagery, body language and gesture. For example, a footballer kissing the club crest on his shirt after scoring a goal seeks to demonstrate not only his belonging to the 'clan' and its shared values (ethos), but also, a love for the club, which is an emotional connect (pathos).

Pathos enables you to impact the mood of your audience, often as a precursor to an attempt to influence their minds (logos) and then their actions. For example, Bob Geldof's anger at the plight of starving children in Ethiopia in 1985 helped create a worldwide emotional response, which he built upon through reasoned argument (logos) to persuade people to act and donate. Geldof's anger and the way it was expressed were natural and genuine and spoke eloquently.

Always try and anticipate the likely emotional response and attitude of your target audience. Such preparation makes it more likely that you'll adopt the correct approach. For example, in my role as a mediator trying to help people settle disputes, I always try to assess the likely emotional response of people in the negotiation – will it be anger, frustration or sadness? I then adopt the appropriate strategies to manage those feelings so that they do not unduly obstruct the mediation process.

Once the mood of the audience is detected, the speaker can adopt the appropriate response. For example, Barack Obama's positive and upbeat 'Yes We Can' presidential campaign in 2008, during which he used positive and optimistic language (such as exciting, historic and transformational), contrasts very much with President Trump's negative 2017 campaign, which fed on the anger and frustration of many white working-class Americans.

You do not need to be a psychologist to understand the range of emotions that are likely to impact someone's mood or decision-making process. Simply watch a television advert and note how emotions such as fear, jealousy, joy and sadness clearly inform the work of the advertising agency.

Emotional appeals can be exploited by organisations to differentiate themselves from competitors. I recall a discussion with a marketing partner from a leading law firm who was concerned that his firm's reputation as being 'friendly' might put off potential clients who considered such a culture to be a sign of weakness.

An understanding of our target audience's values and belief systems, will help predict how people are likely to respond to our arguments. For example: an advocate making submissions will be mindful of the court's obligation to interpret the law in the interests of fairness and justice; someone pitching on Dragons' Den would be well advised to have in mind business 'values', which rarely have any connection with fairness and justice!

Identifying and then keeping in mind your audience's values and belief systems helps you create and maintain a coherence that is likely to appeal to them (see ethos appeal).

A.4.2 Gauging the mood: understand to be understood

Before we can begin to influence people's mood or actions it is first necessary to establish their existing emotional state. This is often the speaker's first task.

For example, how do you prepare for someone who is emotionally charged, perhaps angry and upset? Someone who feels they have been treated poorly by your company and wishes to complain? In business, you'll often need to speak to someone who might be considered awkward, challenging or simply difficult.

In such cases, you should resist mirroring the emotion, for instance, reacting with anger to anger. Such an approach only creates disengagement – or worse. Nor should you be too quick to profess that you 'understand', as it is very unlikely that you *truly* understand, and a crude attempt at empathy is in danger of sounding patronising. In my work as a listening volunteer with the Samaritans I avoided telling a caller that I understood their despair or distress because it could come across as insincere and risk alienating the caller.

However, Bill Clinton managed to engage with a whole nation in his 1992 presidential campaign by telling them 'I feel your pain'; while Donald Trump's 2016 campaign seemed to do little more than tap into people's anger and frustration.

Perhaps it is easier to empathise in such a personal way with a large group than it is with an individual. Illustration A.11 demonstrates a masterclass in how important it is to be able to talk to the audience's mood and emotion.

Illustration A.12 Advocacy watch: Bobby Kennedy on the assassination of Martin Luther King

On 4 April 1968 Bobby Kennedy was due to speak in Indianapolis in support of his presidential nomination campaign. As his plane touched down, he was told that Martin Luther King had been assassinated. He was advised that his safety could not be guaranteed if he proceeded to the rally, which was being held in the heart of an African-American ghetto.

Kennedy ignored the advice and, from a flatback truck, bravely delivered a short speech of great clarity and conviction calling for peace. At that time, most of the crowd had not heard of the assassination.

Kennedy appeased the audience by empathising with them. He talked of King's assassination by a 'white man', he explained that he shared that anger having had his own brother slain by a 'white man'. Having created a connection (ethos) in this way he was then able to quote some poetry by Aeschylus, which talks to reconciliation love and compassion.

Indianapolis was one of the few cities in the USA that did not riot that night.

A truly great speech by a great man who was tragically assassinated a few weeks later.

Illustration A.13 shows how the emotions of your audience can sometimes be managed by a carefully crafted concession or admission. It also illustrates how it is often best to offload bad news as soon as possible, which gives you some prospect of assuaging your audience's anger and re-engaging.

Illustration A.13 Advocacy watch: dealing with an angry audience

One morning I had to make an application before a judge to vary a timetable that he had ordered earlier in the litigation. My problem related to the production of witness statements, which were due to be filed within two weeks – I needed another month!

The case before mine was almost identical, save that the lawyer was seeking a short timetable extension of about a week. Imagine my horror when the judge tore into the hapless advocate, telling him that 'it was just not good enough' and that 'court timetables were to be adhered to and taken seriously', they would only be varied in the 'most exceptional circumstances'. After a ferocious telling-off, the angry and red-faced judge reluctantly granted the advocate what he was seeking. It was now my turn!

I decided to 'fess up' straight away and began, 'My Lord. May I begin by saying that I have been in court during the last application and that I have noted very carefully all you have said to my friend Mr. X concerning extensions of time. I wish to make this particularly clear My Lord as my application is very similar to my friend's, save only that I am required to seek a further month.'

The judge, although furious, recognised that I understood his frustration and, albeit with some reluctance, gave me the order I sought without tearing me off a strip in the process.

We have seen that before you can begin to persuade or engage with your audience (be it an individual or a nation) you first have to *understand* and *empathise* with them. Are they angry or fearful or just bored? Once you have a fix on their emotional state you can respond, not by copying or imitating their behaviour, but by demonstrating that you are aware of how they feel. This in itself is engaging and is a first step toward *talking to and not at*, a crucial element of persuasive behaviour that is dealt with in Chapter 20.

Illustration A.14 Try this: ascertaining the mood

If faced with an emotionally charged audience, be it a colleague or a customer, try and find out how the situation is impacting upon their feelings. As always, some subtlety is called for and it would be foolish to ask a clearly angry individual how they were feeling about a situation. However, in less obvious situations, such as talking to a colleague about work issues, the following questions can provoke interesting responses that will help you address the problem.

1. 'You said last week that you were not enthusiastic about the takeover. Have you had any change of heart?'

2. 'How are you feeling about this development?'

3. 'What would you feel about settling the claim today?'

A.4.3 Change the mood

In the previous section we looked at how one should try and gauge the mood of an audience. Pathos concerns how we can try and change the audience's mood to engender a greater level of engagement, to make them more attentive to our message or argument.

The secret here is to try and create a degree of *intimacy* with your audience. By demonstrating that you know something about their culture, shared values or common sentiment you demonstrate that you know them. You can see from this point that there is an overlap between developing a pathos appeal and demonstrating ethos credibility. Again, it is important to remember that Aristotle's three pillars of persuasion – ethos, pathos and logos – do not stand-alone and each element impacts in some way on every occasion we speak.

Illustration A.15 Advocacy watch: 'And of course Jim liked his throat pastilles...'

Despite getting the deceased's name wrong throughout the service, the vicar redeemed himself and brought a smile to the face of the congregation by demonstrating that he knew of Jim's (very) strange passion for throat pastilles – which warmed his audience's mood by demonstrating that he knew something personal about Jim.

The throat pastilles reference was far more revealing and intimate than Jim's passion for Doncaster Rovers and the Labour Party. It showed that the vicar had done more than a cursory stocktake of Jim's life in his preparation. He was thus able to build up a good ethos appeal with his audience and use an emotional reference to warm his audience. A clever vicar!

The same sort of intimacy can be achieved in the commercial world by ensuring that you do more than read the press releases and websites of large client companies. Ask yourself what you know about the inner workings of the company and their culture? Clearly judgement is required here – you do not wish to frighten away a potential client by looking like a stalker. Nor do you want to raise something that could cause embarrassment. However, an awareness of cultural mores and attitudes can build a rapport and a good engagement as demonstrated in Illustration A.14.

Illustration A.16 Advocacy coach: understanding your audience's values

Most companies wish to differentiate themselves by defining what they allege are their **values** (part of their ethos appeal).

One of my clients was obsessive about her firm's values and prescribed that any training should make specific reference to them at every opportunity. Frankly, this was overkill, and I was concerned that the lawyers I was training might consider some of their values rather platitudinous, or simply 'management speak'.

I overcame this problem by first making reference to the values in a **slightly** pejorative tone: 'Of course, I know that your corporate values are very important to you guys here at X&Co.' This predictably and immediately created a knowing mischievous smile from many of the delegates, who were no doubt bored to death by their evangelical HR Director waxing on about values at every opportunity. I had created a slightly conspiratorial pathos connection with the group. Having raised the issue in this informal and apparently offhand way, and having managed the mood, I was then able to deal with some of the value points in a more productive way.

I began by asking why some of the group had smiled in the way they had. A sensible and very enlightening discussion ensued that resulted in a concern being raised that there was an apparent disconnect between the values as espoused and the behaviour of the organisation in practice.

A.4.4 Tell a story

A speaker can make an emotional connection with the audience in many ways, but perhaps the easiest is to tell a story (see Chapter 19). Often, a speaker uses storytelling to introduce their background and credibility (ethos), creating some emotional connection at the same time.

Illustration A.17 Advocacy watch: Plan B's Ted Talk

Ben Drew, aka Plan B, a rapper and hip-hop artist, gave an excellent Ted Talk when he spoke about how teachers at his referral school in Inner London helped him adopt a more positive attitude to things and how this nurtured his interest in music and helping disadvantaged children. To engage with his audience, he began his speech by candidly telling the story of his own disadvantages and early schooling.

A story or anecdote can often be used to link your objective to a triggered emotional response from the audience. The story structure can help steer the audience through the proposals, conclusions and arguments.

Illustration A.18 Advocacy watch: evoking anger

I once applied to a judge for a committal order (imprisonment) against a landlord who had blatantly failed to comply with two previous orders he had made. I began by summarising the case history and reminded the judge that he hadn't hesitated to grant orders on my two earlier applications, after he'd heard of the landlord's shocking behaviour and harassment.

Then, in the form of a story narrative, I told the judge how the landlord on both earlier occasions had demonstrated a 'blatant disregard' for the court by failing to comply with any part of the judge's orders. This had caused an elderly and infirm tenant a great degree of stress and anxiety, of the type the judge had contemplated when he had made the orders. My emphasis on the landlord's cavalier attitude and apparent contempt for the judge's order, and the impact this behaviour had upon an 'octogenarian war hero' seemed to work. Barely containing his fury, the judge immediately committed the rogue landlord to prison for his flagrant contempt.

A.4.5 Share an emotion and engage your audience

By establishing a shared emotion with an audience an advocate ensures that they become more active listeners. In such cases the audience is more likely to act in the way that you invite them to act. However, success is not always guaranteed, as is evident in the response of the American legislature to the gun control arguments raised by President Obama following a school shooting (see Rhetorical Masterclass at section A.8.3)

Illustration A.19 Try this: how do you feel about ...

Many people are brought up to suppress their emotions. For example: boys are sometimes told that they should not cry; professional and business people can sidestep a consideration of emotions when making decisions or analysing situations. Some say that emotion has no part to play in business, which is a rational (logos) world. Although there is much to support the argument that logos should trump pathos, that does not mean that pathos should be ignored. Often, 'peeling back' a little and asking somebody how something made them 'feel' opens up new avenues and provides real insight into how a problem should be tackled. Certainly, as a mediator I often ask people how an occurrence made them feel and the resulting indicator of an emotional perspective enables me to make progress.

Illustration A.20 Try this: inflate language to heighten emotional impact

Experiment with semantics to gauge the impact that carefully chosen words can have in evoking an emotional response.

The alliterative 'Help for Heroes' is a much more compelling demand than a simple request to assist retired soldiers.

To suggest that somebody 'abandoned' a project is more likely to elicit an emotional response than a suggestion that they simply 'left'.

Reference to a 'compassionate carer' suggests a greater contribution than reference to a simple 'helper'.

A.5 Logos: Appeal to Rationality and Reason

A.5.1 Scope of logos

Logos and its approach to building a reasoned and compelling argument was looked at in some detail in Module B. This section offers a broad overview and an explanation to distinguish it from the other pillars, ethos and pathos.

Ethos measures the speaker's impact on the instincts of the audience. Pathos relates to the role that emotions can play in changing the mood of the audience. Logos, the third pillar, concerns the role of rational argument in persuasion.

Logos concerns the way in which an argument is constructed and the extent to which it is rational and logic. For example, to what extent do the facts and reasoning make your argument more intellectually compelling than your opponent's?

It is important to bear in mind the pragmatic nature of logos, focusing as it does on persuading and not unduly concerning itself with trying to establish the truth.

The inductive nature of rhetorical argument means that assumptions, generalisations and analogy all play a part. For example, an argument that 'all bankers are greedy and will leave the UK if forced to pay higher taxes' is built on a number of assumptions and generalisations, yet it still appeals to a rational analysis. When coupled with pathos – perhaps relating to 'huge bonuses' while still being 'propped up' by the taxpayer – the anger of the audience will make the logos argument even more compelling. Get a former Chancellor of the Exchequer to make the argument and it becomes even more persuasive.

A.5.2 Commonplace

A *commonplace* is a shared piece of experience or wisdom that creates some intimacy or connection with an audience.

It can be specific in a cultural sense or of more general application, such as a truism, proverb, adage, maxim, or even a platitude or cliché. For the technique to work it only matters that your audience 'gets it'.

A commonplace is often used to signpost the direction of travel, or thrust of an argument. For example, a speaker who starts with the adage 'Hard work deserves reward' is probably going to argue about fairness, perhaps adding 'a fair day's work deserves a fair day's pay' for good measure. Not only will such a device signal the central thrust of the argument, it also says something about the speaker's values, thus addressing their ethos appeal.

However, beware of using commonplaces that are overworked and/or clichés. Apart from irritating your audience there is a risk that your quick-witted opponent will produce some equally bland maxims to counter your opening remarks. For example, any advocate who starts with a commonplace such as 'Many hands make light work', deserves to have his opponent respond with 'Too many cooks spoil the broth'.

Commonplaces can go beyond clichés and tired maxims. The key is to remember that they relate to a knowledge of things that are shared between speaker and audience. They might be a company custom or a religious practice. They may even be something racy, like a joke about a perceived institutional oddity. Clearly, take great care in making jocular references in the form of commonplaces when they relate to sensitive matters.

A.5.3 Facts and figures

A rational argument is underpinned with facts and figures, evidence and data. For example, consider how advertising agencies use this approach to make their claims sound more likely. One great example is an advertisement that builds on the ethos or reputation of the car manufacturer Audi which begins by asking the rhetorical question 'What makes an Audi?', it then bombards us with so much statistical data relating to testing and quality control that you are left with the overwhelming impression that the car must be of the highest quality imaginable.

Advertisers also use words that are suggestive of the quality of the product or service being promoted. For good examples of this look for any advert that purports to compare a company's broadband performance with a competitor. Note such words as faster, maximum or better, which in this context probably count for nothing!

A.6 Rhetorical Modes: Strategies for Sorting Stuff

A.6.1 Introduction

Rhetorical modes are simply strategies for deciding how we should separate out and present 'stuff'. They enable us to frame things in a way that makes it clear to our audience whether and when we are arguing, as opposed to simply explaining.

Rhetorical modes apply equally to speaking and to writing skills as they enable us to be more structured, clearer and in control – as seen in Cicero's advice on structuring a speech (see Chapter 17)

Illustration A.21 Advocacy coach: Speech structure and applicable rhetorical modes

Cicero suggested that a speech should be separated into five segments. The first four segments illustrate the different rhetorical modes (in italics) discussed in this section:

1. **Introduction** to the topic (exposition and/or description)

2. **History** or context (*narrative*)

3. **Issues** that are to be argued (*division*)

4. **Arguments** to be made (*argument*)

5. **Peroration** (the *summary*)

A.6.2 Exposition: the introduction

The art of expounding, setting forth and explaining is primarily intended to convey information or to explain. Exposition is different from argument, when reasons are given to support ideas, actions or theories.

An *exposition* should objectively inform, instruct or present. Sometimes this is achieved by *description*. Examples are: a newspaper reporting facts established at an inquest; a work colleague instructing someone how to use a coffee machine; and a policeman giving someone directions to a venue.

When in exposition mode the speaker should be objective and factual. The audience should feel they can rely on what's been said. At this stage, the objective is to inform, not to spin or influence.

In the context of a dispute, a well-delivered and skilful exposition can help the speaker build ethos appeal by engaging and informing the audience in a neutral way, prior to presenting the arguments.

Illustration A.22 Try this: separating out contested facts from agreed facts and framing

In the context of a dispute, perhaps in a negotiation, a skilful advocate can preface comments to separate out disputed content from agreed matters. For example, 'I would like to set out what I understand is agreed between the parties before we move on to the disputed matters and begin the negotiation.'

The advocate builds ethos appeal by ensuring that the **exposition** or **description** is factual and objective.

A.6.3 Narrative: the context

A narration or a narrative provides an opportunity for the speaker to give a short history of what has happened. Think of it as a chronological list of events.

Generally, a narration is required when your audience knows little or nothing about the events concerned and where such a history will enable them to make sense of further issues. As with Exposition and Description the advocate must take care to be objective and not stray into 'argument'. Illustration A.23 shows the difference between narration and argument very well.

Illustration A.23 Advocacy watch: Keir Starmer at the assisted dying debate

As a former Director of Public Prosecutions (DPP) Keir Starmer had direct experience of the decision-making process on whether to prosecute people alleged to have played a part in a third party's suicide. Indeed, he had drawn up the guidelines. In light of this, as Keir Starmer MP he began his contribution to the House of Commons Assisted Dying Debate in September 2015 with the history (narration) of his experience as DPP.

'May I lay out for the House the history of the guidelines that I issued and my experience in operating them? I am well aware of the deeply held views on all sides, and very respectful of them, as I have been throughout the past seven years. I will therefore attempt this exercise as a factual chronology, objectively stated, so that people can see the conclusions that I have reached.'

When asked 'to give way' (i.e. allow another MP) to interrupt, Mr. Starmer replied:

'For the reasons I have given, I genuinely think it may be more helpful for the House if I just completed the exercise. I am deliberately trying not to put my views into this chronology so that people can simply see it for what it is, whatever view they take... I hope that I have been faithful to my obligation to try to put this in a neutral, objective way, setting out the position.'

Only when Mr. Starmer had finished his **exposition** and **narration**, outlining the factual position, did he move on to his **argument** in support of the Bill to allow assisted dying. This movement from one rhetorical mode to the next is called **transition** and this important advocacy skill is discussed in Appendix B.4.

Illustration A.24 Try this: objectivity

When in **exposition** or **narrative** mode, take care to emphasise that you are being non-partisan and objective. When reporting events, preface and frame your comments with an indication that you are going to deal with the history, as you **understand** it. By framing things in this way, it will not matter so much if you are subsequently corrected on a point.

For example, 'Perhaps it might help at this stage if I set out my understanding of what has happened here...'

A.6.4 Division: setting out the issues

This mode concerns the setting out of your argument(s), or stating your case. Aristotle suggested that each argument has two distinct parts. First, the advocate must 'state their case', that is, spell out what it is they wish to argue, *before* they proceed with the proof or argument itself. It helps to think of it as setting out your agenda and articulating the issues.

For example, in opening a criminal case a prosecutor will set out with great clarity the facts that are relied upon and the charge that stems from those facts – this is the division. Once the charge has been spelt out the prosecutor then proceeds to the evidence and arguments that they claim will establish guilt.

The division in a non-legal context is when the advocate sets out precisely what they wish to argue. In most day-to-day arguments there is some freedom to define the argument to suit your agenda and objectives. For example, a chair planning a meeting should consider the framing and order of agenda items that are likely to be contested and argued over.

Illustration A.25 Try this: and your point is?

When unfocused argument or squabbling breaks out it can indicate that people are missing the point, or that they don't have a point.

In such cases, and without being aggressive or sarcastic, try and focus people on the issue they should argue (or that you want them to address) and move away from simply shouting at each other.

1. 'It seems to me that the central point we have to decide today is...'

2. 'I'm sorry, but I'm not precisely clear what your point is.'

A.6.5 Argument

In contrast with a fact-based exposition or narrative an *argument* is a point of view or opinion.

Although a narrative can tell us who has won the FA Cup over the last ten years and an exposition can enlighten us as to who the team members of the 1966 England World Cup winning team were, only an argument can address who was the greatest footballer of all time. Likewise, only an argument can help us determine what was (probably) agreed between two business people who now have radically different recollections of terms agreed some time ago.

The structure of the argument depends upon the nature of the matter being debated and the advocate's strategy. Often, an advocate simply presents an opinion and then offers reasons and premises in support. For example, I might wish to argue that Pele was the best footballer of all time on the basis of three reasons: a, b and c.

Another argument may require a more complex structure. For example, if I wished to argue that the UK should have stayed in the EU, I might wish to begin with a brief history (narration) of UK economic growth since we joined, which may also require citing facts and figures (exposition). Having laid out the background I then need to spell out precisely what I wish to argue (division). I might focus on national security or build my argument on economic grounds, or I might choose both. Precisely what I decide to argue is part of the division process. However, having set out what I wish to argue (division), I need to persuade my audience to my point of view, which is when the argument mode kicks in. Detail on the content and strategies of argument are in Module B and in Chapter 18.

Illustration A.26 Advocacy coach: rhetorical mediation

An inexperienced mediator told me she was having problems. Although she felt able to retain some degree of control at the beginning of a mediation meeting it wasn't long before things 'kicked off' and the parties began to shout at each other.

I advised the mediator that it was worth imposing a clear structure and agenda from the outset and to make sure of a clear distinction between different rhetorical modes.

For example, at the beginning she should set out a clear and comprehensive **narrative/exposition**, during which she should emphasise that she was dealing with what she understood was the history and common ground between the parties, that is, the facts. If she had to refer to a contested issues (e.g. who did what and when) she should make it clear that the point might be contentious by saying, 'I believe the claimant's case is she gave notice on 10 February, while the defendant has no recollection of having received notice at any time.'

A clear demarcation between modes helps to make it clear to the parties that she is in control of the facts and mindful of their separate arguments. This approach also enables her to emphasise the history that has been agreed between the parties – the common ground.

Then she can move on to the **division**, the summary of the contested points. Again, these should be couched in a way that is acceptable to both parties.

After this stage – and not before – she can invite each party to present their **argument**, within a time limit and without any interruption from the other side.

Illustration A.27 Advocacy coach: rhetorical diagnosis

Let us imagine how a junior doctor might collect their thoughts about a new patient before reporting the situation to a senior consultant.

They might begin by setting the scene in **exposition** mode, including details of how the patient presented at casualty, with reference to facts such as symptoms, temperature, blood pressure and laboratory test results.

At that stage they might move on to **narration**, with a brief history of the patient's condition, before moving on to **division** – in this case, setting out their view of what the patient might be suffering from.

Having identified a condition (e.g. pleurisy or diabetes) they'll be ready to move on to the **argument** mode by setting out the reasons in support of the diagnosis.

A.7 Tense: Power of Time Travel

A.7.1 Introduction

Why do some arguments end up in heated disagreements? Because the parties are stuck in the wrong tense.

If you want to control an argument and make progress it helps to know when and how to switch between the three tenses. Aristotle advised that we should always be mindful of what tense we are arguing in and referred to them as:

- Past tense – judicial
- Present tense – demonstrative
- Future tense – deliberative

A.7.2 Past: judicial

When we argue in the past tense it is generally to address blame. For example, who 'screwed up' or who is responsible for a state of affairs. This is the tense that is often heard in a court of law.

If blame is an issue you should concentrate on arguing in the past tense, with an historical analysis and evidence to support your arguments. For instance, in an argument over the sacking of a football manager, John said: 'Well, he's only got himself to blame! The results have been a disaster. Let's look at his record. Last season he only won five times and so far this season we haven't won a game.'

A.7.3 Present: demonstrative

This mode is concerned with the here and now and is best used to address values and what might be considered as 'good' or 'bad'. It is often used in eulogies.

Martin Luther King dedicated his life to love and
to justice for his fellow human beings, and he died
because of that effort. In this difficult day, in this
difficult time for the United States, it is perhaps
well to ask what kind of a nation we are and what
direction we want to move in. (Senator Robert F.
Kennedy on the assassination of Martin Luther
King, Jr., Indianapolis, Indiana, 4 April 1968)

But values are not restricted to eulogies. Let's consider what
Sue says in response to John's critique of the sacked football
manager. 'It's not just about results John. My point is that he
was given a six-year contract and this has been reneged upon
by the club. I can't believe that a club with the standing and
reputation of United could have behaved in such an unethical
and unprincipled way; they even leaked news of his dismissal
before they told him! And how did they tell him? By text! The
owner's behaviour shows no class nor any common decency.'

There is rarely any useful point served, in arguing the
toss, about whether something is 'good' or 'bad' or 'right' or
'wrong', and Sue's venting is unlikely to make much difference
to the argument about whether the club were right to sack the
manager. However, if her objective is to focus on the issue of
the club or its owner's credibility and/reputation then such a
focus can play a part in reflecting their ethos appeal or lack of it.

A.7.4 Future: deliberative

In our football argument it is Jane's turn to contribute:
'Come on Sue, climb off your moral high horse. What has
happened has happened and there is no point going on about
who's to blame, or whether the club has behaved well. The
interesting thing is, who are they going to sign to replace him?

My money is on Menger – he'll make a great boss. And I'll give you three reasons why my money is on him...'

Jane does not want to dwell on the past, or argue about virtue and principles; instead, she looks to the future and addresses the choices and options that are *now* open to the club. This focus on future tense generally involves discussions leading to decisions, that is, arguing about choice.

A.7.5 Practical pointers: tense

As you prepare an argument or speech it is a good idea to separate out the materials and your notes so that different tenses are dealt with in distinct and separate sections and you do not muddle them up. The importance of structuring and organising your material is addressed in Chapter 16 Organisation.

Switching tense is a powerful rhetorical tool as it enables an advocate to maintain control and to change focus to a more productive topic. The technique is shown in Illustration A.26.

Illustration A.28 Try this: switch tense to introduce another issue

If you're stuck in an argument based on values or blame, reframe it to the future and to questions of choice. This can involve 'hiving off' issues, that is, putting things such as blame to one side and refocusing on solutions:

'Clearly, we need to establish all the facts and who is to blame in due course, but for now I suggest we focus on what we are going to do about the situation as we move forward.'

Reframing an argument to reflect on another issue can help to keep things moving. For example, this argument about the morals of tuition fees is getting stuck. Move it by focusing on a different (although related) question:

'OK, I don't think we're going to agree about whether it is fair that tuition fees should be paid by the government, so let's move on and look at whether people – as a matter of principle – are prepared to pay taxes to fund other people's education.'

The following two illustrations offer further examples of how a focus on tense can create positive results. The first relates to a study on ways of getting people back to work and the second is a hypothetical story about two warring chefs.

Illustration A.29 Advocacy watch: research tense

A government organisation conducted research into how to get people back into work. In one trial job seekers were asked to outline what they were planning to do within the next two weeks in relation to finding a job. This approach replaced the old system in which job seekers were asked what steps they had taken in the previous two weeks. This change in emphasis, plus some psychological support, created impressive results, with 15%–20% of applicants more likely to get off benefits.

The Behavioural Insights Team Blog, 'New BIT trial results: helping people back into work', 14 December 2012

Illustration A.30 Advocacy watch: future choice

As a commercial mediator I'm aware of how people involved in litigation are often stuck in a time frame, generally the **past**. The temptation is to embark on an expensive process that airs their competing views of history before a court. In due course, a judgment is given and one party wins and one loses.

An important element of mediation, as an alternative to litigation, is getting the parties to focus on the **future**; to look ahead and discuss plans and ideas that often have no direct connection with the issues between the parties. These incursions into the future enable the parties to consider new options that would not have arisen had it not been for the informality of the mediation process.

The following story concerns two chefs in a busy kitchen who fall out over an orange they both claim to own. They are so incensed with each other that they instruct law firms to prepare legal arguments that support their ownership of the orange. If the matter goes to court the orange will rot, but at least the chefs will have their day in court and receive a judgment that resolves the argument one way or another.

Imagine that instead of going to court the chefs agree to mediation. Each one meets separately with a mediator, who asks them not to dwell on what has happened in the past and why they believe they are entitled to the orange. Instead, the mediator asks them to explain **why** they need the orange. During a judicial/forensic process, **need** is not generally a relevant consideration as the focus will be on legal questions of **entitlement** and **ownership** and identifying the facts that facilitate a judgment. However, as a result of the private meetings, the mediator establishes that Chef A needs the orange flesh to make a fruit salad and that Chef B needs its skin/zest to bake a cake!

A deal is done quickly and the chefs praise the power of focusing on the future and on the issue of choice.

A.8 Rhetorical Techniques and Masterclass

A.8.1 Introduction

In the previous sections of Appendix A we looked at some rhetorical insights and strategies that are universal in their application and relatively straightforward and easy to understand and apply.

This section looks at a few rhetorical devices that are less strategic but equally worth knowing. The ones I've chosen are quite mainstream and are best considered as a rhetorical 'starter kit'. Experiment with them as often as you can and, once you're familiar with them, you'll recognise how commonplace the techniques are. Sections A.8.3.1 and A.8.3.2 are rhetorical masterclasses from two famously skilled speakers.

A.8.2 Classical rhetorical techniques

A.8.2.1 Repetition (anaphora)

An anaphora simply involves repeating a word or short phrase in speech (or writing) at the beginning of a clause or sentence. It is an extremely useful device to build rhythm and emphasis into what you are saying.

One of the most famous and well-known examples of anaphora is Martin Luther King's 1963 Civil Rights Speech in which four key repeated words – 'I have a dream' – addressed his vision of the future (see A.7 Tense) with great pathos, lifting the spirits and hopes of a generation of Americans.

Do not think anaphora is restricted to high-level rhetoric. Repetition can be used in all manner of situations where you wish to highlight or accentuate an important point.

A.8.2.2 Lists (asyndeton)

The technique of simply listing things can add cadence and rhythm to your speech.

The dropping of conjunctions such as 'and' can speed up your delivery so the words used support your key point. This technique is often coupled with the use of anaphora (repetition) as demonstrated by Churchill listing the locations where 'we shall fight' Hitler:

> *We shall go on to the end. We shall fight in France, we shall fight on the seas and oceans; we shall fight with growing confidence and growing strength in the air. We shall defend our island whatever the cost*

*may be; we shall fight on the beaches, we shall fight
on the landing grounds, we shall fight in the fields
and in the streets, we shall fight in the hills; we shall
never surrender (Winston Churchill, 4 June 1940)*

This quote was also looked at in Chapter 20 Engagement.

Illustration A.31 Try this: summary by list

Use a list to summarise the key points in a pitch or negotiation. In this example additional emphasis can be given by pointing to and counting off the points on your fingers.

'In summary, if you choose to engage us you will have 24-hour cover, competitive rates, partner input, biggest presence in UK, ...'

A.8.2.3 Answering your own rhetorical question (hypophora)

This device is much-loved by politicians who wish to get key messages and points across by answering the very question they would like to be asked: 'How are we going to tackle inflation? I have three points...'

You can use hypophora to structure your pitch or presentation speech. The technique is not so useful in an interview or a conversational setting, when you might be accused of speaking at and not to your audience.

Illustration A.32 Try this: answer the question your audience wants answering

In opening a presentation or when called upon to speak for a short while, begin by stating a carefully crafted rhetorical question. This technique works if you pose the question that your audience wants to hear an answer to.

'Amid all the press speculation, the people want to know whether I propose to resign. Let me answer that question directly...'

A.8.2.4 Timing (kairos)

Many arguments fail as a consequence of their timing. Knowing when and in what way to advance an argument is part of an advocate's skill and kairos is the rhetorical term that relates to the phenomenon of what is the right or opportune time to advance a particular argument.

Kairos explains why holiday companies advertise heavily in the New Year, why charity appeals are more successful following a disaster – and that canny timing of young children asking their parents for favours or treats.

Sometimes an argument has to be advanced when there is little prospect of engagement or influence, but the point still has to be made. Winston Churchill's warnings of the dangers of Nazism and the rearming of Germany in the 1930s often fell on deaf ears and his voice only began to make its mark in a wider sense after the war began in 1939.

On a practical basis, kairos is important in deciding when to make your rhetorical move. For example, if there is some customary squabbling during a meeting it is often best to sit on your hands and 'bide your time'. When no progress is being made, then you intervene and summarise your understanding of 'where we are', and offer up a sensible proposal which people will be keen to support – if for no other reason than to keep things moving. The same sense of timing can be used to coincide with a change in the mood of your audience. As we have seen, people's attitude to certain appeals will depend upon their mood (pathos) and the best time to strike in a rhetorical sense is when the mood changes.

Illustration A.33 Try this: take control

Take control by questioning the timing of the question or of a proposed argument: 'I realise that we may need to discuss how much we pay them, but today we should first determine whether we have any obligation in the first place.'

A.8.2.5 Irony (paralipsis)

This is a common rhetorical technique of referring to something by claiming not to refer to it. It is much-loved by politicians and those who operate in adversarial and challenging environments, where it is often important to attack the credibility (ethos) of your opponent.

Illustration A.34 Advocacy watch: Boris Johnson

In this short section from a speech given by Boris Johnson before the London Olympics in 2012, note the way he begins by referencing his American origins (he was born in New York) in an amusing way to suggest that he would not wish to tease his hosts (ethos) before going on to do just that.

'As a native New Yorker, I will resist the arid, chauvinistic, claptrap about the supremacy of London. It would be indelicate to suggest that London has more top 100 universities than any city on Earth, more top law firms, more top PR firms, more international tourists than any other city in the world and an economy twice the size of Denmark. I am certainly not going to stand before you now and crow about the triumph of Billy Elliot in the Tony awards. And far be it for me to rub in our success at winning the Olympic games.'

Johnson has used paralipsis in a fun way, but it can also be deployed in more serious situations, when the speaker wishes to allude to something without being too specific. For example, an advocate who says, 'I am not suggesting he was drunk' is implying that alcohol might have had some bearing upon someone's judgement. If you do use paralipsis like this there may be ethical considerations and you may be asked to clarify, 'Exactly what are you alleging?' In such a case, a speaker risks damaging their ethos appeal if, for example, it is established that the individual concerned had only had one drink.

Illustration A.35 Try this: use of hypothesis

A less direct way of inferring something is to use a hypothesis, such as, 'Many may have formed the view that he was bullying.'

Using the technique in this way offers some protection from an accusation that you are personally attacking the ethos of another. Of course, there are still ethical considerations and a badly judged smear can rebound on the speaker's reputation.

A.8.2.6 Think three (tricolon)

Three is a great number to bear in mind as you plan what you want to say and how you are going to say it. For example, saying, 'I have three points', suggests that you have considered carefully what you want to say and that there is some discipline to your approach. On the other hand, the advocate who says 'I have loads of things to say' suggests that he is going to make it up as he goes along.

Using this well-known rhetorical technique, speakers structure sentences in three clearly defined parts. There is no shortage of memorable tricolon quotes – here are three:

1. 'Never in the field of human conflict was so much owed, by so many, to so few.' Churchill

2. 'I came, I saw, I conquered.' attributed to Julius Caesar

3. 'government of the people, by the people, for the people, shall not perish from the earth.' Abraham Lincoln.

Although you may not anticipate having to deliver a Gettysburg address any time soon, it is very useful to learn and to practise this technique. It need not appear overblown or exaggerated to focus on three elements and their cheek by jowl articulation can make your argument more engaging, persuasive and memorable. It also delivers a rhythm that is easier on your audience's ear.

A.8.3 Rhetorical masterclass

This section refers to two pieces of advocacy from two very different advocates, at very different times, and for very different ends. They provide good examples of much of the material in this appendix and I recommend that you check out the actual speeches in online videos.

A.8.3.1 George Galloway: 'Oil-for-Food' Senate Enquiry 2005

In May 2005 George Galloway was summoned to appear before the US Senate Enquiry that was investigating allegations of breaches of the UN's Oil-for-Food Programme. This programme permitted Iraq to avoid sanctions by selling oil when the revenue was to be used to buy food and medicine.

It had been alleged that George Galloway, a vehement anti-Iraq-War advocate and an MP, had personally benefited from sanction breaches and, as a consequence, he was summoned to appear.

The following is an extract of Galloway's opening and bullish remarks following the laying out of charges by the Chair of the Senate, Norm Coleman. I note in italics where rhetorical techniques have been used.

- I am not now, nor have I ever been, an oil trader (and neither has anyone on my behalf). [*denial/refutation*]

- I have never seen a barrel of oil, owned one, brought one, sold one (and neither has anyone on my behalf). [*list – asyndeton*]
- Now I know that standards have slipped over the last couple of years but for a lawyer you are remarkable cavalier with any idea of justice. [*ethos attack*]
- I'm here today but last week you already found me guilty. You traduced my name around the world without ever asking me a single question, without ever having contacted me, without having written to me, or telephoned me, without any contact with me whatsoever and you call that justice? [*repetition – anaphora; past tense (blame); rhetorical question?*]
- Now I want to deal with the pages that relate to me in this dossier and I want to point out areas where there are – let's be 'charitable' – and say errors. [*irony; ethos attack*]
- On the first page of your document about me you assert that I have had many meetings with Saddam Hussein. This is false. I have had two meetings with Saddam Hussein [dates] on no stretch of the English language can that be seen as many meetings with Saddam Hussein. [*refute; attacks exaggeration*]
- As a matter of fact, I have met him exactly the number of times Donald Rumsfeld had met him [*analogy*] the difference is that when Rumsfeld met him, he met him to sell him guns, and maps the better to target those guns. I met him to try and bring about an end to sanctions, suffering and war [*tricolon*] and on the second of those occasions I met him to try and persuade him to allow Dr Hans Blix and the UN weapons inspectors back into the country. A rather better use of two meetings with

Saddam Hussein than your own Secretary of State made of his [*ethos*].

Comments

'I am not now...' By exploiting primacy, Galloway begins with a clear denial of any suggestion that he has profited from oil sales. He is unequivocal in this regard and focuses on the denial by switching tense from the present to the past. Galloway also seems to be aware of the danger of *pregnant denial*, which occurs when a denial can be construed as a form of admission. For instance, 'I have never shoplifted from Boots' could imply that I have shoplifted elsewhere. It is with this in mind that Galloway sensibly states that 'neither has anyone on my behalf'.

'I have never seen a barrel of oil...' Galloway uses a list (asyndeton) and logos to underpin his claim that he is not involved in oil trading.

'Now I know that standards have slipped but for a lawyer, you are remarkably cavalier with any idea of justice.' Galloway goes on the attack by questioning the credibility of the Enquiry and its Chairman through their failure to contact him, to give him a chance to respond to the charge.

'without ever asking me a single question...' is great use of anaphora (the repetition of without) and a rhetorical question ('you call that justice?')

'I want to point out areas where there are – let's be "charitable" – and say errors', still on the ethos attack, Galloway uses irony with his concession that inaccuracies could be mistakes, while the implication is that these could have been falsehoods. By being 'charitable' he seeks to enhance his own ethos appeal.

' "many meetings" this is false...' is a crystal-clear refutation of an exaggerated allegation. Once exposed, this further weakens the credibility of the report and the Enquiry itself – a great example of the dangers of exaggeration.

'the same number of times as Donald Rumsfeld' is a great use of analogy.

'I met him to try and bring about an end to sanctions, suffering and war', this use of tricolon emphasises the positive nature of Galloway's meetings, as compared to Rumsfeld's selling of guns.

A.8.3.2 Barack Obama: Sandy Hook School shooting

On 14 December 2012, Adam Lanza shot dead 20 children and 6 teachers at the Sandy Hook Elementary School in Connecticut. Later that day President Obama made a short speech to the nation. There is often reference to the tear he wipes from his eye, but this outward display of pathos and heartbreak is only a small detail in a remarkable short speech. The President first evokes his ethos as a parent before going on to speak in an emotive way (pathos) during which he seeks to signpost the arguments that need to be made (logos).

- We've endured too many of these tragedies in the past few years. [*commonplace*; *logos*]
- And each time I learn the news I react not as a president, but as anybody else would – as a parent. [*ethos*] And that was especially true today. I know there's not a parent in America who doesn't feel the same overwhelming grief that I do.
- The majority of those who died today were children – beautiful little kids between the ages of 5 and 10 years old. [*pathos*] They had their entire lives ahead of them

- – birthdays, graduations, weddings, kids of their own. [a*syndeton*]
- Among the fallen were also teachers – men and women who devoted their lives to helping our children fulfill their dreams.
- So, our hearts are broken today – for the parents and grandparents, sisters and brothers of these little children, and for the families of the adults who were lost. [a*syndeton*] Our hearts are broken for the parents of the survivors as well, for as blessed as they are to have their children home tonight, they know that their children's innocence has been torn away from them too early, and there are no words that will ease their pain.
- As a country, we have been through this too many times. [*logos*]
- Whether it's an elementary school in Newtown, or a shopping mall in Oregon, or a temple in Wisconsin, or a movie theatre in Aurora, or a street corner in Chicago Asyndeton – these neighborhoods are our neighborhoods, and these children are our children. [*ethos*] And we're going to have to come together and take meaningful action to prevent more tragedies like this, regardless of the politics. [*logos*]
- This evening, Michelle and I will do what I know every parent in America will do, which is hug our children a little tighter and we'll tell them that we love them, and we'll remind each other how deeply we love one another. But there are families in Connecticut who cannot do that tonight. And they need all of us right now. In the hard days to come, that community needs us to be at our best as Americans. And I will do everything in my power as President to help.

Comments

'We've endured too many of these tragedies...' Obama begins with a commonplace and an appeal to logos or rationality, while at the same time reminding his audience that he is qualified to speak on this occasion as a parent, thus boosting his credentials or ethos.

'The majority of those who died today were children – beautiful little kids between the ages of 5 and 10 years old.' A heart-rending reference to the victims, followed by a list (asyndeton) of the events that have been stolen from the children.

'As a country, we have been through this too many times. Whether it's an elementary school in Newtown, or a shopping mall in Oregon.' Again, Obama reverts to a logos argument and uses asyndeton to list evidence of other such events to remind people why they have suffered these disasters 'too many times'.

'these neighborhoods are our neighborhoods, and these children are our children. And we're going to have to come together and take meaningful action to prevent more tragedies like this, regardless of the politics.' Obama repeats 'our' before reverting to the rational need to take action 'regardless of politics'.

Appendix B •
Presentational Tips

These notes provide a useful precis of the things an advocate should have in mind as they prepare to present their argument. Including a note for those who have a problem with anxiety.

B.1 Getting Off the Starting Blocks

The psychological concept of *primacy* suggests that people are more likely to listen attentively to what we say at the beginning of our presentation. This means that we need get off to a sound start and create a good initial impression.

To help manage initial anxiety, know precisely how you are going to begin, and make a note of the exact words that you plan to use. Knowing what you are going to say when you start means you can rehearse and practise your opening and thus lessen the risk of creating a bad first impression.

Try and keep the first few sentences 'safe' and free of controversy. Unless you are an entertainer do not try a stand-up routine. Just get on with what you want to say, keep it simple, and try and build a rapport with your audience – the jokes can come later.

B.2 Creating a Good Impression

As many people have said, 'You never get a second opportunity to make a good first impression'.

What can you say at the outset so your audience warm to you?

Try and have some discussion or contact with your audience *before* the presentation. For example, find out what their attitude is to some of the issues being addressed and/or their expectations. Referring to such discussions during your speech demonstrates that you are properly prepared and that you are mindful of and care about their attitudes, interests and concerns. Such discussions will also give you confident that you are addressing things that your audience want you to address. It is also comforting to have started the 'conversation' and broken the ice before you begin in a formal sense.

As we have seen, ethos appeal depends upon your audience believing you are knowledgeable. Telling them this can risk showing off. The solution is to be subtle. Perhaps put some reference to your achievements and qualifications in your pre-presentation briefing and/or get someone else to introduce you and show off on your behalf. Universities introducing visiting speakers are very good at this – and can go on for some time about how wonderful the visiting speaker is!

B.3 Creating an Agenda

It is often sensible to exploit an old adage:

- Tell them what you are going to tell them
- tell them
- tell them what you have told them.

This is particularly useful when you have an information-heavy exposition. For example, in a presentation relating to business change the speaker could continue after his introduction: 'I am here today to advise you of the changes that we will be introducing over the next couple of months. I shall begin by outlining some of the problems we have been faced with over the last couple of years before I set out what operational problems we need to address. Then I will explain the decisions we have taken to address these problems. There will be an opportunity to ask questions at the end of my presentation and unless any one has any questions at this stage, I will begin by addressing the history and the problems that have led to these changes.'

Setting out what you propose to deal with and in what order, enables your audience to have a preliminary overview of your arguments, or case. This can aid their understanding and prevent them interrupting you by, for example, asking questions about issues that are going to be dealt with later. This structure is very useful in formal situations, such as submissions to a court or tribunal.

B.4 Transitions: Moving From One Section to Another

A lawyer will always be concerned to keep people on the 'same page'. The best way to do this is to tell them when you are going to 'turn the page'. This advice is consistent with the aim of always talking to your audience, and never at them (see Chapter 20 Engagement).

The easiest way of disengaging your audience is by talking too fast and not pausing. One way of engineering pauses is to stop at each 'transition point'. Think of this as a place where you 'take stock' before you move on from one section/subject to another. Note how a skilled chairperson will summarise at the end of each agenda item and then move on to the next topic.

This is an extremely useful technique providing you have an opportunity to summarise before inviting your audience to ask questions.

In the above example, at the end of the narrative on why there had been problems our speaker will wish to move on and address the issues that have been identified and will need resolving in the future. This requires a shift in tense, from past to future. To make the shift from one subject (and one tense) to another quite clear, the speaker must make the transition quite clear.

In smaller groups and less formal presentations a transition provides a great opportunity to ask if there are any questions. Such a technique allows the speaker to look at the audience and assess their engagement.

Planned transition points are also an opportunity for the speaker to summarise the topic dealt with in the preceding section prior to moving on to the next.

B.5 Let's Get Physical: Body Language

There is plenty of advice on the internet about how you should use your body language – some more interesting/relevant than others. This section focuses on just six issues that, in my experience, are essential to keep your audience fully engaged.

B.5.1 Am I looking, really looking, at my audience?

It is hard to listen to someone when they are unable or unwilling to make eye contact with you. Although we do talk on the telephone we generally find communication is easier with those we know or when the exchanges are routine. However, if we have a deal to negotiate, a proposal to make, or a lesson to teach it is generally best to sit down and discuss things 'eye to eye'.

Eye contact is essential, whether you are talking to the nation via a camera, to colleagues in a Zoom meeting, or to an individual across the boardroom table. If you are talking to a group, make sure that you 'range' around. Don't ignore anybody or concentrate on a few. This ranging around the room can be disconcerting, as some members of your audience may look bored, distracted or even incredulous at what you are saying. It is very easy to assume that they are disinterested – and they may be – but you must never give up on them.

I always try and identify the friendly 'nodder' in the audience – the one who smiles sweetly at you and nods at everything you say. These people are a great comfort to nervous speakers.

B.5.2 Am I fiddling?

Fiddling does not matter, unless it distracts you or your audience from what you are saying. If you are looking at your audience you will generally be able to pick up on any signs of disengagement. For example, people will look at the clicking pen in your hand, or notice that you are fiddling with change in your pocket. If they are distracted, stop doing it. Videos of presentational training are a good way of picking up annoying fidgets.

Illustration B.1 Advocacy coach: body language

One of my colleagues was told that she had a problem with 'fiddling', which distracted her audience. I watched her on a video review and she seemed to be in a constant state of fidget: pulling at her hair one moment, twisting her ring the next, before picking up her pen and clicking the end. She was a serial fiddler and I could imagine how this might distract and/or annoy her audience. Her fiddling emanated from her nervous energy and it was hard for her to stand still.

My advice was to practise vigorously twiddling/scrunching her toes as she spoke. This is both subversive and effective. Your audience has no idea what is going on inside your shoes but these hidden and frenetic movements seem to satisfy the fidget habits of the most serial fidgeters.

B.5.3 Am I standing up straight?

An open, confident and positive stance will evoke a belief in your audience that you are confident and positive. It also help your breathing and, according to Amy Cuddy, accelerates your own self-belief and confidence. Her excellent 'fake it until you make it' advice is included in her well-worth viewing talk, 'What we tell ourselves with our body language' (TEDGlobal 2012, 28 June 2012).

One tip is to stand with your feet a shoulder width apart and then point your toes inwards in a 'pizza' shape ski position. Try it and you will notice that standing like this helps you feel grounded and stops you swaying from side to side. This stance also ensures that your torso is leaning forward at the correct angle. However, overdo it and you run the risk of looking a bit silly!

B.5.4 Are my hands shaking?

Decide what you are going to do with your hands before you stand up. This is similar advice to deciding what you are going to say before you stand. If it's appropriate, hold a notebook with one hand and a pen with the other. If your hands shake, get a heavier notebook or pick up a book with the same hand. The weight will stop the shaking and you get a good work out at the same time!

Another technique is to use a lectern and place your hands on either side. If you do take comfort in fiddling try holding a pen but make sure it is not a clicking one. I use a pen to tick off items in my notebook as I proceed.

B.5.5 Dry mouth?

Water! Have a bottle and glass to hand.

B.5.6 Memory lapses

Keep a list of items you intend to address and then at each transition point simply tick off the item you have just dealt with. If at any stage you lose your way, just stop. Do not try and wing it, or 'um' and 'er' your way through the embarrassment. Simply say, 'May I just have a moment please?' Then look at your list and see what point you were up to, take stock, and – when you're ready – start again. Take as long as you need to collect your thoughts. Your audience will not mind. In 40 years of public speaking I have never had an audience say that I could not have a moment.

B.5.7 How do I sound?

Stand straight, lift your head up, pull your shoulders back and focus your initial attention on those furthest away from you.

There are many other problems that may impact upon how you sound, from having a quiet voice to a stammer. There are few issues that cannot be successfully addressed and my advice is to search for specific advice and guidance.

Some people ask how they should deal with their accent or dialect. My usual response is to ask them why they feel it is necessary. Provided their accent is not so distinctive that it distracts or the audience cannot make out what is being said, it should not be a problem. However, if you are not happy with the way you sound then it is sensible to do something about it. A voice coach can help moderate the way you speak – Margaret Thatcher sought help from a voice coach. One way to improve is to read out loud a passage from Shakespeare or a poem. Learn one by heart and it is also a good warming-up exercise, as is the speaking aloud of tongue twisters.

B.5.8 Plan how to finish

It is often sensible to engineer a Q&A session toward the end of the presentation. This allows people to clarify issues. However, it is best not to finish on a Q&A session as enthusiasm can peter out. Instead, pick up the tempo and finish on a high note with a quote or short story that illustrates many of the points you have made.

B.6 Nervous?

A speaker will always have clear objectives in mind: a leader may seek to inspire; a teacher to inform; and a comedian to entertain. There is *always* a risk of falling short and this fear of failure *should* make any speaker nervous.

Illustration B.2 Addressing nerves

Two renowned advocates had to address their nerves: Churchill and Cicero.

Churchill was not a natural orator. Indeed, he was nervous to the point of nausea and was hampered by a stammer and a lisp. He mastered his nerves by dint of hard work.

This quote from Cicero – considered by many as the greatest orator ever – evidences that even the good and great can be nervous and anxious, but can overcome their nerves through practice and a desire to improve.

'Indeed, I am always very nervous when I begin to speak. As often as I rise to speak, so often do I think that I am myself on trial, not only as to my ability, but also as to my virtue and as to the discharge of my duty; lest I should either seem to have undertaken what I am incapable of performing, which is an impudent act, or not to perform it as well as I can, which is either a perfidious action or a careless one. But that time I was so agitated, that I was afraid of everything. I was afraid, if I said nothing, of being thought utterly devoid of eloquence, and if I said much in a case, of being considered the most shameless of men.' M. Tullius Cicero. *The Orations of Marcus Tullius Cicero*, translated by C.D. Yonge, B.A. London. Henry G. Bohn, York Street, Covent Garden 1856.

Typical manifestations of nerves are:

- blushing
- fidgeting
- shortness of breath
- hunched body language
- lack of eye contact
- blanking out and forgetting your way
- talking too quickly
- dry mouth.

Each of these anxiety manifestations can be actively managed and eradicated. In any event, many of the perceived anxieties are not a problem. For example, fidgeting, sweating, or even forgetting your place is not itself a problem – unless and until it begins to distract the audience or the advocate, from what is being said. Many of these manifestations have been addressed but one further issue does need mentioning – speed.

A real issue for nervous advocates is that they often speak too quickly. This is a problem as they can end up talking at and not to their audience, which is a complete turn off.

Fortunately, pace can easily be resolved. The suggestion to 'slow down' is not helpful. The solution is to engineer specific pause points in your presentation. If you have created an agenda or a list of topics ensure that your notes clearly remind you when you can effect a transition. These points enable you to summarise and then ask if the audience has any questions. Another opportunity to pause is to refer to a passage you want to read out.

If time permits (and particularly if you are anxious) it can be sensible to prepare a full script of your speech. Then you can run through it and practise your delivery. However, a script should be the starting point and it is sensible to work on preparing a separate list of bullet points, each of which reflect discernible 'chunks' of your presentation, including appropriate sub headings. Such notes will facilitate the use of transition points.

It is also extremely helpful to prepare a short synopsis, a few words about what you intend to convey. This is often a difficult task!

Think twice before deciding simply to read your script. Unless you are an accomplished actor, it is extremely difficult to engage your audience while reading to them. There may be sections where it is appropriate to refer to your script (e.g. to read out a quote or some evidential findings) to support your argument or for emphasis. Having sections marked out to read verbatim gives some variety to your presentational style, and can be a welcome break for both you and your audience – especially if the text is likely to be well received by the audience.

Illustration B.3 Advocacy coach: function of a prepared script

A colleague agreed to deliver a eulogy at a friend's funeral. He knew what he wanted to say but he was worried that he'd falter or lose his way and wondered whether he should simply read from a script.

My advice was that he should keep a copy of the script close at hand that he could refer to in 'case of an emergency' (e.g. if he froze or lost his way). Then I gave him advice on how to prepare bullet points that he could write on cards. I also encouraged him to build in some quotes he could read off the cards. The use of cards facilitate a more engaging presentation.

The fact that he had the script to hand, and the knowledge that he would be able to read some of the quotations, gave him the confidence to rely solely on his cards.

Illustration B.4 ends this section with opportunities for a 'nervous' advocate to develop their confidence. Like most things, it is a question of practising and of juxtaposing confidence with competence.

Illustration B.4 Developing confidence and competence

If you still feel anxious or lack confidence, take every opportunity you can to practise being assertive. Take a more partisan view next time the opportunity presents itself, for example, complain in a restaurant or return shoddy goods to a retailer.

Work on articulating precisely what you want, don't be vague. Say, 'I want a complete refund' not 'What are you going to do about this?'

Practise shutting up! Put your point across, keep it short and wait for a response. Resist the temptation to keep talking. Silence is indicative of confidence and is part of the advocacy process. It is a particularly useful technique to use in negotiations.

Engineer more silence and gaps in your day-to-day discussions. This can be done quite easily. Once you become more mindful of the pace at which you speak in normal situations, you will be able to adapt more easily to stressful situations. You will also become a better listener.

Appendix C •
Top Tips

C.1 Interviewing or Questioning a 'Witness'

This appendix supplements Chapter 2.

1. Begin by building up a clear picture of the factual background; the uncontroversial stuff that is unlikely to be disputed. These agreed facts generally outnumber the contested matters and cover chronology, locations, timings, people involved and so on. These agreed facts are the bedrock, or context, of your case. Indeed, the bulk of a lawyer's case consists of *agreed facts* and an advocate who can express these clearly before moving on to contested matters is more likely to have the ear of their audience. Setting out matters in a non-partisan way is a crucial presentation skill.

2. Bear in mind when someone recounts their experiences they tend to be selective and wish to focus on the contested or disputed issues and the arguments they want to make. Try and avoid too much of a focus on contested matters at the beginning of your investigation. Put them to one side, to be returned to once you have a broad and reliable picture of the background and the facts leading up to the dispute.

3. Be mindful that the 'map is not the territory'. Keep an open mind and recognise that the explanation you are listening to is unlikely to be the whole truth, it is

generally an individual's best effort at recalling the past. When reporting your understanding to third parties be very careful to frame, or qualify, your findings to reflect this. For instance, 'Douglas has a pretty good recollection of events and is very sure that he reported the problem to the contractor. He is very experienced in these types of contracts and I think his recollection is very reliable.'

4. Listen carefully and tease out and clarify qualitative and judgemental statements such as 'It was a lovely day' and 'I think he did a good job'. What do people mean by such statements? (See Chapter 4 Questioning and Active Listening)

5. Watch out for assumptions, generalisations, cause and effect conclusions, and other potential weaknesses in the reasoning process. (These techniques are also dealt with in Chapter 4 and in discussions of the reasoning process in Module B)

6. Watch out for and note inconsistencies between different witness accounts. By all means seek clarification, but do not encourage them to remember things in a different way in an attempt to 'polish the evidence' and/or make the recollections 'fit' together. 'Coaching a witness' (as lawyers call it) nearly always ends up reducing the reliability of that account. The fact that people remember things differently is only to be expected. It is much better to focus on the common ground between witnesses, as this is more likely to reflect what did happen. Lawyers are relatively relaxed about inconsistencies between witnesses and do not assume that inconsistencies destroy the credibility of the case. On the other hand, a lawyer will look for

inconsistencies in opposing witnesses and, if they are serious, will focus on them in cross-examination to devalue their credibility.

7. Beware of incorporating your own words or summaries into a witness account just because you believe you can express it better! Although it is sensible to moderate things where necessary by qualifying a witness's assertions with 'To the best of my recollection', 'In my opinion', or 'It is my belief that'. Only use hard frames such as 'It is a fact' or 'It is incontrovertibly the case', when you are confident that such assertions cannot be refuted.

8. When recording someone's opinion it is sensible to refer to the facts that led to the forming of that opinion. For example, instead of just recording 'It was a lovely day', include such facts as 'There was no rain, the temperature was in the mid-twenties all day, there were no clouds in the sky; it was a lovely day.'

9. Remember that people are more often 'mistaken' than 'lying'. It is perfectly correct (and not at all aggressive) to suggest someone may be mistaken. However, if you believe that they are lying, it may be necessary to formally challenge their account of events by calling them out, that is, tell them that you believe they are wrong. A less confrontational way of challenging a witness is to suggest that their account may be challenged by cross-examination at a later time and ask them how they'd respond to a suggestion that their account was dishonest. In this way you are not personally challenging the witness.

C.2 Interviewing or Questioning a Reluctant Witness

What happens when you seek help from someone who – for whatever reason – does not want to help? Think of them as the 'No comment' person being questioned by the police.

In such cases you have to decide whether to persist with or to abandon your investigation with such an individual. Much will depend upon the potential importance of their contribution. Their account may be crucial and you may have to put pressure on them to assist. It helps, at least at the outset, to keep any exchange as short and factual as possible and to focus on eliciting uncontentious information. You can often get some movement from a reluctant witness by getting them to agree a series of uncontroversial facts. For example, asking them to confirm their understanding of a chronology of agreed dates and times'. Once some common ground has been 'agreed' and the witness has opened up, they may then be more inclined to speak openly about more contested points.

Another technique is to 'feed' the witness some third-party accounts. This technique can provoke a response from someone who has previously declined to contribute.

C.3 Determining Issues

1. Issues should be crystal clear. For example, if someone complains that your people have provided a 'sloppy service', you should ask them precisely what they mean. If you wish to raise a complaint you should, as lawyers say, fully 'particularise' your allegation. Breaking it down into its elements, each of which could become an

issue. For instance: delivered the wrong order; to the wrong depot; and not within contractual dates.

2. Try and use facts in your allegations as these will build a context and are unlikely to become issues.

3. When considering a third party's claim consider what parts you can concede and what parts you have to deny; it is the disputed elements that form the issues.

4. When trying to resolve a dispute – perhaps at a meeting – seek to agree precisely what you disagree on. If possible, set out these issues before the meeting to focus preparation and save time later.

About the author

Following a period as a senior law lecturer Simon returned to private practice and spent ten years as a litigation lawyer and partner in two leading City law firms. It was this commercial experience, coupled with his teaching skills, that led to him becoming sought after to provide training and coaching to other lawyers. As a consequence Simon left full-time practice and has since focused on running training programmes to help lawyers sharpen their skills in argument. In 2018 Simon extended his offering to provide coaching and training to those outside the legal profession who wished to develop their advocacy skills.

Simon presents workshops, on-line training and consultancy – all tailored to the client's requirements. His 'Argue like a Lawyer' workshop is a popular session and is based on some of the key points in this book. He also enjoys helping and coaching non-native English speakers, and those who lack confidence and resilience or who suffer from nerves.

As part of his passion about the role of advocacy Simon enjoys creating interesting training interventions to enhance existing development and training programmes.

When not working he can be found playing football, visiting art galleries or walking his dog.

For further details about Simon's career and offerings please visit:

LinkedIn
simoncoathconsultancy.co.uk

'People still remember and talk positively of Simon's 'Argue like a Lawyer' workshop held two years ago!'

Jeff Belk, BSc. (Hons) FRICS, Head of Estate Projects, University Hospital Southampton NHS Foundation Trust, 2021

Index